The Long Way To Happiness

Clara Cruz

&

Kelly Silva

Published by Prime Publishing Studio

Edited by Nikki Lorenzo

Printed in the United States of America

"Only I can judge myself.

I know my past, I know the reason for my choices, I know what I have inside. I know how much I've suffered, I know what it's like to be strong and fragile, me and no one else."

Oscar Wilde

"Cada mano que toco mi piel

Cada paso que dieron mis pies

Cada paisaje que miraron mis ojos

Cada palabra que me emociono o hirio

Cada cancion que escuche

Cada amor o desamor

Dieron vida a este libro."

C.C.

This labor of love is dedicated to all who dream to write their life story and share it with the world.

"*For My Father*"

Contents

Fica (my great grandmother) Me at two years old and Lola (my mother)

Prologue

Last night, while swinging on our hand-carved rocking chair, carved by a local Amish in our town, on the balcony of the second-story cabin home pondering the beauty of a full moon in the snowy mountains of North Carolina and while in deep conversation with my feisty granddaughter, Nikki, who holds an immense love and passion for writing, as she is a professional writer, asked me,

"Mama, por que nunca se te ha ocurrido de escribir un libro de la historia de tu vida?"

I thought about her question for a beat before replying,

"Yes, many times I've thought about writing a book about my life; it certainly has all the elements to create a world where I would be seen, heard, and understood. I better do it now; after all this year I'm turning 70, and my memory is already fading, but I'll consider the idea."

Excitedly, Nikki shared,

"You don't even have to do anything in chronological order; simply start writing chapters of events that you remember and have impacted your life, then later you could put them in order."

Over the next few days, I began seriously thinking about her idea, but thought, *why would people run out to read my life's story?* After all, I'm not a celebrity, successful figure, or life coach, wherein people would be interested in my story. Then I began to ponder the fact that everyone certainly has a story to share about their life and maybe mine could help others write their own. I ultimately convinced myself, and thus slowly began the agonizing process of venturing into a writer's journey. I outlined a plan to dictate my life's story throughout the years and convinced my daughter, Kelly, who loves to create, write, and produce, to transcribe my ramblings into a book; she excitedly accepted the challenge. I managed to dictate and record important chapters of my life in my native language, Spanish — as I'm originally of Cuban descent, on a small, old, broken-down recorder I found discarded in a drawer. Although it was challenging to allow myself space and share intimate situations that had never seen the day of light, until now, I felt vulnerable and unsure how people would react. Eventually, I found the courage to sit down and express even those difficult moments, hoping I could inspire others, and in the process found healing. I cautiously emailed it in sections to Kelly, who had commenced the tedious task of translating them from Spanish to English and structuring the recordings in a way that would make for an interesting read. My hope is, perhaps, to inspire the uninspired to seek out their happiness in this life and challenge them to create a life worth writing about.

Being an avid reader allowed me the opportunity to seek out the happiness, awaiting me in this life, in other places around the world. I was introduced to the novels of Corin Tellado published in "*Vanidades,*" a famous fashion and news magazine in Cuba, established in the 30s when I was barely 10 years old. I immediately found myself strangely addicted to reading adult magazines and then later yearning for a taste of real authors, such as Hemingway, Emily Bronte, Honore de Balzac, Edgar Allan Poe, and Arthur Conan Doyle, to name a few. Unbeknownst to me, reading blossomed into an undiscovered avenue for me to escape my current reality and explore the beauty of living someone else's life; it was an escape and yet also a determination. The more I grappled with writing my life story, the more I realized I did, in fact, want to share it.

I also believed that sharing my story might help my family better understand me and the choices I've made along the way. As a Cuban immigrant, loved ones would be able to picture my

3

personal Latin upbringing and the difficulties I had to over-
come and the obstacles thrown along the way, which in turn
molded me and shaped me into a woman. Maybe then they
would understand; maybe then they would forgive me and love
me, regardless of all the difficult decisions I've had to make,
which have ultimately changed them as well.

Introduction

Life in Cuba, at least for me, began somewhat unconventional; my parents divorced when I was a year old and detested each other. I was tossed around households and schools my entire young life— this created a sense of utter loneliness within me. It didn't help that I was constantly shuffled around between relatives, sometimes having to stay with my resentful mother and other moments spending time with my absent father, continuing until I was 11 years old. My father, Elias, was a genius in his own right while my mother, Lola, was cold and unloving: only later in my life did I come to understand her and her sadness. I spent most of my time with my grandmother Naty, (my father's mother) and with my great grandmother and my great aunt, who was my godmother on my mother's side. The rest of the time, I was living in a convent, lonely, scared, and unloved for a period of four years.

Throughout this book, I will sporadically introduce some of the people who guided my journey, one way or another, in finding myself and happiness; and those who played an integral part in leaving their mark within me, whether it was good or bad. Some I've loved, some I've wanted, others I've needed, those I've used, and some I've longed for. I'm no different from everyone else, *always searching for love, for eternal love; for happiness, eternal happiness.* There have been countless times throughout my life wherein I've asked myself, *what is love?* Was I capable of loving in my loneliness? Has it been various sentiments I've found within each different person I've been drawn towards and not an internal love? I've sacrificed for them, as they have for me, and yet I still find myself asking the same question.

"Am I happy?"

All of these people created a helpful environment in my walk, and I've accepted their love in my own way, but none more than Sergio. He comes in later, keep reading.

Through these pages, you will also experience life in Cuba in the 1950s, how I survived living in an all-girls Convent, the Cuban crisis, Miami, Chicago, and Puerto Rico through my eyes— eyes that always chased after love, family and happiness. Something I never had growing up.

I do believe we all have a story to tell; we all have moments in life that have dictated the inner fibers of our personality; the mold which broke during life's journey and created us as we are today. I'll share the most difficult, the saddest, the cruel, and sometimes the beautiful moments that have encompassed my life in hopes you can also learn to understand your own legacy; a legacy worth sharing. There will be candid moments that have never been shared, not even to my most loved ones; moments I sometimes wish not to recall but find in some way therapeutic to share.

Let us begin.

The Lonely Convent Girl

The all-girls Catholic Convent marked the saddest and un-happiest time of my young, innocent life. I was barely four years old when my father decided to enroll (dump) me in the Convent, a strict all-girls Catholic school consisting of only nuns and priests. According to my dad, since my mother had remarried, he blatantly refused to acknowledge the fact that I had a stepfather by dragging me away, with my mother always gladly accepting; I suppose that it was convenient for her at the time since she after their divorce married a younger man, who did not have enough income to support them, let alone me. In my mother's mind, a child would have been a bit of a nuisance. That thought was embedded deep in my soul and ultimately grew roots, rotting all my decisions throughout my entire life. It was extremely difficult for me, only four years old and al-ready living without a home unit, without love or comfort. Af-ter all, it's difficult for anyone, especially a child, to be alone without parents to love and care for. My heart breaks with sad-ness whenever I learn of lonely children in the world. I can feel their pain — a word I'd come to associate with "love".

Me at the Convent with my class

7

The only *"family"* I knew were the group of girls in the Convent, which, by the way, were all strangers, and the nuns, who were drastically strict. All of the days usually began with mass in the small ancient chapel, with a wooden pew and colorful windows, following a small, tasteless breakfast, tedious classroom studies, lunch in the afternoon, and back to our classes. At the end of the afternoon classes, we were taken to the showers, and since I was little, the nuns had the duty to bathe me. Come to think about it, I don't think my mother ever bathed or dressed me. Before dinner, we were allowed to go to the courtyard to run and play. There were no dolls or toys to play with or any friends to go out and run with, no television or music. It was a bleak existence. I believe the reason the girls in the convent would make fun of me was due to how small I was, being the youngest of them all; being bullied became my everyday. I never understood why; after all, we were all there for the same reason. Kids can be extremely brutal and cruel, inasmuch as they can be pure and truthful, but I was resolved to think we all felt discarded in some way or another by life. Once recess was over, we would retire to the damp, colorless mess hall, which was full of several large wooden tables with old kitchenware. Most of the meals consisted of bland and tasteless food. I remember chewing the rubber meat until there was no more juice, and since I couldn't stomach swallowing it, I would throw it under the table. Secretly, I would visualize that the people who had to clean under the table would find all my chewed-up pieces of meat and wondered who did it; that thought made me giggle. I remember that my father would send me packages with condensed milk and chocolate; that was all I would eat (thus creating an eternal love for sweets my entire life- it became my comfort food). Once dinner was over, we were taken again to the chapel to pray. More often than not, I would fall asleep on the oak pew, and the nuns had to carry me to bed.

The nights were horrible; sleeping in a little uncomfortable iron bed that was surrounded on all three sides by white curtains in a room with 20 girls. It was a cubicle that appeared to look like an asylum. If I needed to visit the bathroom at night, I would hold it, as I was afraid of walking through the long, musky, spooky hallway in the dark. To avoid that, I would, many times, just pee on the bed. The consequence that I would endure the next day entailed a drastic punishment by the nuns. I prayed they would forget, but they never did…punishment was every day. Let's remember I was four. This practice caused several unpleasant nights and undiagnosed childhood trauma.

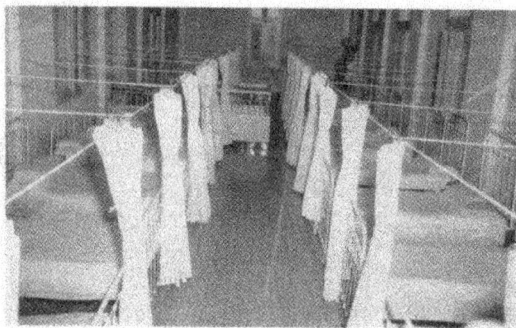

DORMITORIOS PARA INTERNAS
Uno de los amplios y bien ventilados dormitorios del Colegio.

My dorm at the Convent

While living at the Convent, my days were spent alone, scared and depressed. I looked forward to leaving that hell every Saturday morning to go home and despised returning on Sunday afternoons. No child should feel neglected, not by their family, and most importantly, by the world. That day and a half that I spent visiting my mother wasn't memorable, as a matter of fact, she would ignore me the entire time, leaving me to be on my own again. I wondered why she refused to acknowledge my existence, constantly wondering what I did wrong for her to despise me.

When the summer and winter vacations came around, as soon as I would leave the Convent and arrive at my mother's house, there would always be a little brown, beat-up suitcase ready for me on my bed to leave for Havana. My mother and her husband would send me to Havana, and I would be there the entire three months of summer, during which I was split between my paternal grandmother, Naty, and my godmother. The times I was left for vacation with my grandmother at her house, she found me extremely skinny and would cry at my unhealthy sight, thinking I was going to die from starvation. Those three months were the best times of my life, having my cousins to play with at my grandma's house and taking trips to the beach, the zoo, and the movies before returning to Pinar del Rio and the Convent. Those times were the moments I felt a sliver of happiness. When December arrived, the same routine continued; my little brown, beat-up suitcase was ready, and Clara went back to Havana, again to stay in various houses, not one of them my home. I remember crying every time I would return to the Convent and wishing and praying my life would change. I prayed my mother and father would want me, love me, care for me, and ultimately accept me as their daughter. I hoped the girls would stop bullying me; tears soaked my pillow and tore my dreams.

At the age of eight, during one of the trips to Havana, my grandmother shared with me,

"Clara, you are going to stay with me for a few months, and we are sending you to a new Catholic School."

Fortunately for me, this meant I would only stay at the school for half a day and not overnight. I was thrilled. This change only happened because my father returned to Cuba and met a girl in Cienfuegos whom he decided to marry. When he returned from his honeymoon, he rented an apartment in Havana and had me live with him and his new wife, Ela. Ela was a young, inexperienced woman and, again, a woman in my life who lacked a loving hand towards me; although she was pleasant to me, she never displayed real affection towards me. To my dismay, this did not last long since he was transferred to Santiago de Cuba to represent a Venezuelan editorial firm and was going to be distributing books in the Orient province, which was located at the other end of the island. Eventually, my grandmother and uncles would move to my father's apartment for the sole purpose of caring for me during those six weeks until my father established himself in Santiago. Even at that apartment, I felt abandoned and forgotten.

Abuela Natalia holding Carlos (my cousin), Me and Juan Angel (my cousin)

Santiago de Cuba

Me with Elias (my dad), Ela (my step-mother) Eli (my step-brother)

One day, my uncle Carlos Cruz, my father's younger brother, a stubby, happy man who wore a black wig because at the age of 17, his friends played a terrible prank on him and poured hot tar over his head, causing him to lose all his hair never able to grow back, took me on a long trip, which I vividly remember was to Santiago de Cuba. At the time, I was in Havana, living temporarily with my grandma in a small grey stone house with a brick-laid front porch, as I mentioned earlier; I was studying in a catholic school, waiting for my father to establish himself and his new wife, who I had previously met when they were living for a short time in Havana. During that time, she was pregnant with my stepbrother, Eli. When they finally moved to Santiago de Cuba, Eli was born. My uncle drove me to Santiago de Cuba on a trip that seemed extremely long in an old, cramped, dirty bus from Havana. When we arrived in Santiago, I saw that my father, his wife, and my step-brother lived in a cute, little, modern brick-and-stone house located in an affluent area of Santiago de Cuba. My father enrolled me in a different Catholic school, but this one did not require me to sleep there, as I would attend in the morning and return home in the afternoon. I suddenly could envision myself finding happiness, maybe, in this place, maybe.

My cousins Carlos, Juan Angel and me

Life in Santiago de Cuba wasn't as structured as in the Convent, I would say a different kind of structure. There were some major differences; by this time, I lived with an actual family: my father, his wife, and their son. Sadly, I still didn't feel like a member of that family, as I've always felt like an outsider, like the one that never belonged, the odd foot. My father was a man with honorable intentions; I knew he always wanted the best for me. He committed himself to providing me with an exceptional education by enrolling me in prestigious schools; he would pay for private classes in ballet and French, and he even hired a tutor to study with me at home. But, the excessiveness of material things was never enough to compensate for the lack of love, tenderness, attention, or even touch from him. All I ever longed for was a hug, a kiss, even a lovely gesture of any kind. I later came to learn and accept that he expressed his affection for me differently — harshly, and materialistically. He was, at times, a violent man; he was a Spaniard at birth, with hard knocks during his life, which he felt justified his violent character. His beatings would come provoked by my rebellious nature, at times, usually beating me with anything in his hands, whether it was a duster, a belt, or a shoe. I stood my ground and bore the blows. Once at dinner, I refused to eat the fish soup, and he silently leaned forward and grabbed the back of my head, clawing his fingers in my hair and thrusting it into the soup. After that, I don't like soups. He would throw household items toward my head, he would slap me red, and always mistreat me physically and mentally. I never quite understood what I would do to provoke his anger. He would spend time punishing me for anything I would do; things were probably insignificant now, as seen through my adult eyes, but for him were apparently bad. He used to make me write continuous lines on a stack of white paper, saying I should not do this or that, causing my fingers to ache and cramp for days. Aside from writing lines and the beatings, I was always punished for one reason or another; this never stopped. Now you can understand why my life in Santiago was not a happy one. While all this was happening, I never once received a letter from my mother, and the ones I wrote to her were left unanswered. I didn't see or hear from my mother during the three years I lived in Santiago with my father and his wife. All the while, not knowing if she was alive or dead. This emotional trauma left me scarred throughout my entire life. I still carry it, but the load has lightened.

During those three years, my father was involved in the revolution against Batista (Batista was president at the time) in

Cuba. Elias was a devoted revolutionary who helped Fidel Castro's army at the time, as he believed in the cause, only to find out later that it was all a lie. Castro misled the entire Cuban population, executed thousands of Cuban people, and ransacked the entire island, seizing property and personal belongings. Since he was involved in the revolution to dethrone Batista, there was a moment when the Batista government found out what my father was involved with. A friend of his in the government warned my father to immediately escape Santiago because his life was in dire danger, as the Batista army learned my father was helping the revolutionaries. We had to immediately abandon Santiago. I remember my father hastily putting us all in his car, instructing us to only pack the essentials. I was able to pack my clothes (in my trusty brown luggage) and no other possessions, as I had none. We sped towards Havana, fleeing the only home I knew. On the way, we stopped off at Cienfuegos, which was where his wife, Ela's family, lived and where he dropped her and the kids off to be safe; no one knew of this place. That car ride was silent, as they were all scared. By this time, they had another child, my half-sister, Mariella, who was a couple of months old when they stayed in Cienfuegos. My dad continued to drive towards my grandma's in Havana to drop me off. I was confused and didn't quite know the gravity of the danger we were in. My father kept calm, but we could see small pebbles of sweat streaming down his forehead. When we arrived, he instructed my grandmother to send me over to Pinar del Rio to live with my mother in order for him to fly out of Cuba to the United States to sort things out and clear his name. This was an ugly transition for me, not knowing what was happening and only fearing I would be abandoned again; up until that point, my life felt half-lived, and even so, I feared losing it.

Pinar del Rio

Lola (mom) and Antonio (step-dad)

By the time I was 11 years old, I found myself in familiar territory, arriving in a home where I was an unwelcomed stranger. My mother had birthed two boys with her young husband, Antonio, who turned out to be a sweet and loving stepfather. He was gentle and caring, and he was a total softy, quite different from my father. The youngest, Joe, lived with her, and the eldest, Anthony, lived with his grandparents in a town near Pinar del Rio; both would later become estranged and uncaring siblings. My mother was a kindergarten teacher (some would call that "ironic") at that time, in a small old school quite close to the house where we lived, and Antonio was a janitor in a college. I could never picture my mother teaching children; after all, she disliked them. *Or maybe she just disliked me.* They were humble people who worked hard to survive, much like every-one else. I have come to believe that to be the reason why they would ship me off to Havana. I can only assume my mainte-nance resulted as financially unattainable to them, something I knew nothing about at the time but later learned to understand through the years; in the meantime, nevertheless, it hurt me deeply, causing my life to be a heavy burden no one wanted. *I questioned if I even wanted it myself.* This thought still didn't explain to me why they never showed affection towards me, or anyone, for that matter. That household was bankrupt of love. They might have been robots…with their wires crossed and short fuses.

The years I lived in Pinar del Rio with my mother, Antonio, and their kids were far from easy. I was unable to create a lov-ing relationship with them, never saw eye to eye, and constantly argued about everything. I continued with my stubborn, defi-ant nature, carrying insecurities that no one loved me and that no one cared. While living together, I noticed that Antonio, who withstood my tantrums and bad behavior and loved my mother dearly, would withstand her intense personality. He knew she was not an easy woman to live with, but he accepted her because he understood she was a product of her own mis-fortune in childhood; she became orphaned at birth when her mother died on the delivery table giving birth to her — some-thing I believe harnessed her hatred for herself and her kids. He earned a place in heaven for dealing with my mother till her death; this I was certain of.

The day I arrived in Pinar del Rio, my mother immediately enrolled me in a public school; up until then, I had always been in private Catholic schools, including the four years in a Con-vent. I remember the first day of class, she sent me to school with a snack in a paper bag to eat at recess. When it was time to go to recess, and I saw the slew of boys and girls of all ages and cultures, which I wasn't ever introduced to, I experienced a panic attack. I stood in a corner, motionless and crying uncontrollably. Apparently, someone noticed I was going through an episode and called my mother, who came to pick me up and take me home. All the ride home, she was belittling me, angry that I wasn't like normal kids. How could I make her understand that I was afraid, not able to handle things, and needed help?

It was my godmother, Dulce, who was my mother's aunt, with whom my mother lived when she was little. Dulce was considered a soft-spoken and respectable rich woman, the one who cared for my mother's monetary needs. When they informed her of the details of my panic attack, she asked my mother to take me to a psychiatrist. I vaguely remember having a session with him. Apparently, the psychiatrist informed them that I was not emotionally or mentally prepared for being in that school. Dulce ended up giving my mother the money to enroll me in a private school, wherein there were still some boys and girls, but it was smaller classes with kids of families with higher economic positions who could manage my situation. I was there between the fifth and sixth grade. Nothing had changed; I still didn't have friends, didn't know anyone, and felt like an unwanted outsider. Ultimately, little by little, as time would have it, I was able to make some friends; it took some work, and since I spent my years moving from place to place, never allowing any time to establish a friendship that could last or outlast my trauma. I saw it as a race where my trauma was winning in each marathon I ran in life. This needed to change.

At barely 12 years old, I made a friend my age, at school, who slowly became my first boyfriend, the son of a doctor. After a few months of talking, he sent me a message with another girl asking if I wanted to be his girlfriend, and I replied,

"Yes."

I finally experienced some sort of happiness at last, having a friend to confide in. The days his father couldn't send their car to pick him up from school, we would walk hand in hand, about a block from the school to another street where he lived, going up, and I lived opposite, going down. There we would walk a block together, him carrying my books and sometimes holding my hand. When we would arrive at the end of our street, he would walk up to his street and I would head down to my house. This new relationship was innocent and harmless; he made me feel seen and special. One day, one of my mother's friends noticed me walking with him, hand-in-hand, and immediately told my mother. We lived in a small town where everyone knew everyone else. My mother showed up the next day and waited at the exit of the school where she saw me holding his hand, and when we approached the corner, she stopped us, screaming and making a scene in front of everybody around. She warned me that if she ever saw me with that boy, she would send me back to Havana, and I would never see him again. My first boyfriend *and friend* was over before it even began. I cried at night thinking I would never know joy, never have friends again, never have someone to talk to and share my thoughts with. I suddenly became that lonely girl once more.

The Silva Charm

Top Left to Right: Me, Alberto, Carlos, Cuca, Normita, Marta at the end Bottom Left to Right: Gallego, Lola, Yayi, Candito, Luisito

By the time I completed sixth grade and commenced high school, we had managed to move to a house in a newer neighborhood. The house my mother lived in when I lived with her was on an old dirt road, in a different area, although the house was somewhat modern and my mom always kept it immaculate, it was different. She loved to care for her house and kept it overly organized, clean, and beautiful. Images of her cleaning in heels flood my memory. I secretly hoped she was taking care of it for us, and sometimes wondered why she didn't care for us like that. Upon my moving in with her, I began a relationship with the neighbors and their daughters, wherein I was finally able to forge real friends. That new white stone house with a small fenced front porch was next door to the Silva family, a wife, Marta, a kind soul, her husband, Candito, a jokester and their boy, Luisito, who was a year old, along with Marta's sister, Normita, a beautiful tall girl with lovely black hair, who was almost two years older than me. Normita immediately became one of my first best friends, which lasted decades until her untimely death due to cancer. On the next block, a few doors down, in a small house, lived the family of Candito Silva, his mom, and four brothers, of which one of them was Carlos (who later became my husband), the sister Yayi, a happy, free spirit girl who quickly became my best friend, as well. Next to their home, from the Silva family, about a block down from my house, lived a girl who was with me in the Academy Gonzalez, who was JoAnn, who at that time was the girlfriend of Javier Mora — a boy who studied with Carlos and who was a neighbor.

Me, Normita (top) and Yayi (bottom) in 1957

All this time, I was still hiding the fact that I was secretly seeing a boy named Pep until one day when I snuck out of the house with a friend at night to get into a fair in town. When I arrived, I caught Pep riding the Ferris wheel with another girl.

I was devastated; I had a panic attack on the spot and broke up with him that night. I ran crying the entire way home, but since I couldn't go home in that state, for fear my mother would find out the reason why I was crying, I decided to visit Yayi, to continue my wallowing and share my heartbreak with her. Carlos, a thin, tall, good-looking man with blue eyes and blonde short hair, walked into the room where Yayi and I were, saw me crying, and asked her,

"Who is that runt crying?"

She explained that I had a problem with my boyfriend, and he said,

"That little runt has a boyfriend?"

In order to understand me a little better, you need to consider that at that time I was 12 going on 20. I always maintained myself as more mature than other kids my age. Life's experiences and the way I was raised, moving from place to place alone, forced me to mature quite fast. At that age, I already felt like an adult. I was always quite decisive and intrepid; I also loved challenges and winning. I held that very seriously, so much that Carlos ended up being my boyfriend, due to a dare. It pains and weighs on me that I couldn't treasure Carlos as much as he treasured me. I did it, as I said previously, to win a bet against my neighbor. Ultimately, that innocent act changed the trajectory of my life forever. I eventually enjoyed being Carlos' girlfriend, which aided an escape from my family. From my loneliness. Carlos became my first escape. I fell in love with his family. Their love for life and for each other was new to me. They would hug each other, laugh, eat, and dance together. I felt thrilled visiting his house; I was addicted to feeling the love from his mother towards her kids and how wonderful they interacted with each other. They were an extraordinarily close-knit family, enormously happy and entirely caring, and that endeared me to them. I longed to be a member of their family.

My days were centered on his sister and five brothers and his aunt Cuca, who was the angel which helped raise her sister's kids, and their kids, finally feeling like I belonged somewhere. Eventually, my mother, as always, found out that I was secretly Carlos' girlfriend. She sternly lectured

"Listen, I know you have been hiding Carlos. But since he has a good family and is serious, studious, and hardworking, I don't want you to hide around with him."

She added,

"If you want to be his girlfriend, he needs to come to our home to visit you while I am there."

In Cuba, Hispanic parents never allowed their daughters to be alone with a boy. Instead, they always needed a chaperone. That is how a courtship in Cuba was handled. The rules were that a boyfriend would visit two or three times a week, but on specific days of the week, Tuesdays, Thursdays, and, I think, Sundays. He would visit from 8-10 pm, and the visits would be sitting on the couch in the living room or on the rocking chairs on the front porch, merely conversing or sometimes sneaking a hold of a hand, and whenever you could steal a kiss, you would, without the family noticing. It was pure and innocent in those days, allowing us to maintain the relationship for three years.

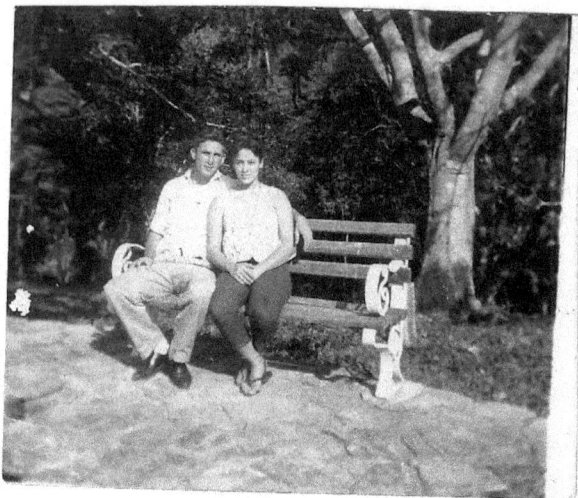

Carlos and Me

Let me take you back a bit before I continue...

When the Fidel revolution triumphed at the beginning of 1959, my father, who was exiled to the United States, returned to Cuba and after being in Havana for a few months, went to visit me in Pinar del Rio. Unbeknownst to me, he was a member of the revolution and working with the government of Fidel Castro at the time. He later confessed to me that he wasn't happy with what was happening in politics, and he knew that the communist revolution was not what he believed to be fighting for, and that he was again leaving the island. Disillusioned, he prepared his trip to exit Cuba again through Venezuela to Puerto Rico. He was merely six months in Havana before he left again. Once he left and established himself in Puerto Rico, he sent word asking if I was interested in leaving the Country, and if so, he would help me get out. Since I was not in favor of the new government of communist Fidel, I told him,

"Yes, I want to leave."

Many Cubans were fooled into thinking Fidel Castro was going to save them and make Cuba a better place to live, but unfortunately, we were all taken advantage of. Once the Communist Party took control of the Country, those who didn't align with the Communist Party were jailed or had their property confiscated. Laws were implemented to keep everyone docile; food was rationed to the bare minimum within families, power was shut off, material items were taken, and the destruction of the Cuban people began in numbers. The government had spies everywhere.

When my father was able to claim me to live with him in Puerto Rico, my mother didn't allow it. Since I was underage, I couldn't leave the island without my mother's permission; I was left behind. I think she must have done this in vengeance against my father for taking me from her without her consent. In retaliation, I decided to ask Carlos,

"Why don't we get married?"

I believed the only way to leave Cuba and be free was to get married. Carlos accepted, solely, I believe, because he also wanted to abandon the island, given the fact that his father was a political prisoner jailed by Fidel Castro for his diligence to the Batista government, where he was a Lieutenant in the army against the Revolution. Our hope was to live free in Cuba, but we were forced to leave our homeland because of a government that we were not in favor of. The things you do to escape.

I forgot to mention that when I was 14 years old, to everyone's surprise, my mother announced she was pregnant with her fourth child. Imagine the shock when I received that news; my first sentiment was embarrassment, because the simple fact that my mother was having sex repulsed me. The second thought was, really, another child, you? It was something I did not want to accept, and I felt ashamed that they would see her pregnant, and never shared the news with anyone that I was going to have another sibling.

When she communicated the news to my godmother, her aunt Dulce, the person who had constantly helped her financially, she also reacted in an alarming state. She wasn't in agreement with having another child at that stage of her life, mind you, my mother was 37 years old at the time, keeping in mind their financial distress. They already had three children with jobs that paid poorly, insufficient to maintain the family they had, let alone support another mouth to feed. My Godmother, as always, came to the rescue and bought everything for the new baby: a crib, sheets, clothing, and everything else. She was a savior.

When the baby was born in November, it was a cute little sweet girl, thus they named her "Dulce" which means "sweet" in Spanish, in honor of my mother's aunt Dulce, who was the family's benefactor. When little Dulce was born, we all fell in love with her, being the new toy in the house. I remember when my mother returned to work, I took care of little Dulce and even me only being 14 years old saw her as my first child. Although her birth was unexpected, it was ultimately a blessing. She lived her entire life with my mother and her husband, caring for them throughout all their illnesses and ultimately till their death.

Infatuation Speaks Louder Than Words

What I'm about to share in this chapter is known only to a select few, and I hesitated to share it when the book idea came to me. However, ultimately, I felt that this story was important to share for reasons that each person will see differently.

It was around Valentine's day, I was about 14 years old and barely in a relationship with Carlos when one day I was walking down Calle Real, the principal street of our town where all the town's shops were lined up; as I often did because the school I attended was at the opposite side from my house on that street; I would walk Calle Real every day four times a day to and from school going home because we would go to school in the morning, return midday for lunch, and go back to school again in the afternoon, then back home. During one of those trips to school, I stopped at a little store, a gift shop called *"La Casa Crystal."*

Calle Real

On the window display, I noticed a set of cute cufflinks for sale. I decided to get them for Carlos as his Valentine's gift. I entered the interesting store, and behind the cash register was an older man who attended to me quite nicely. I explained to him my interest in the cufflink set on display and how I wanted to give it to my boyfriend as a gift. He looked at me and said

"Muchachita, Tu tienes un novio?"

I responded,

"Si, yo tengo un novio y quiero darle eso para Valentine's. Pero no tengo mucho dinero. Cuanto es?"

I explained why I wanted them, but I had no money. I asked him if I could pay in installments, and he smiled,

"Yes, let's see what we can do."

We began chatting about life when he casually asked who my family was. I mentioned to him I was the daughter of Lola Suero. He said in disbelief.

"You are Lola's daughter?"

I responded with a nod,

"Yes."

He went on,

"I'm a close friend of your mother, as your mother and I went to school together. I care dearly for her. Please let her know Tomas sends her greetings".

He continued with,

"Let's do something so that you can buy that set for your boyfriend."

I was left quite impressed by him. As you might have realized, Tomas was my mother's age; he was 23 years my senior, but in my mind, I was an adult. I was 14 going on 40. I remember arriving home that day, excitedly turning to my mother,

"I met Tomas at the store he owns. He said he was your friend from school."

She happily replied,

"Yes, we went to school together. Next time you see him, give my regards."

Shortly after, I began stopping by the store daily on my way to school. I made sure to always enter with the excuse to make a small payment for the cufflinks, but in reality, I yearned for our long and interesting conversations.

Strange thing, through time, I believed I worked up a little crush on Tomas. I knew it was something totally impossible, but nevertheless, I was intrigued by him. I tried to speak with Carlos on various occasions to share my feelings, but I was afraid of what he would think of me. I secretly wanted to tell him, but my fear of losing him and his family was too great. I felt Carlos noticed something different with me, but I felt he didn't want to come to terms with the outcome, whatever that may be. I decided to share my feelings towards Tomas with my mother, thinking it would help my situation, but to my dismay, she rejected any feelings for him, explaining the circumstances in order for my young mind to understand. In a chilling tone she muttered these words that I will never forget.

"Estas montada en el burro y tienes que darle los palos."

If the situation doesn't suit you, but you have no other alternative, you are forced to act against your own desires.

Needless to say, I was fascinated with Tomas; he was mature and sophisticated, with a welcoming smile and stimulating conversations, and he was truly interested in me; he *saw* me. He was an adult who would talk with me as if I were at his age, and perhaps in my naïveté mind, I thought I was. After I made the last payment of the installments for the famous set of cufflinks, I needed an excuse to keep going to the store to keep speaking with Tomas; through him I enjoyed learning about life. At the time, I had a beautiful pearl ring that my aunt Celia had gifted me, which was one of my most treasured possessions. The ring had a shiny pearl lifted in the air from the band, and one day, I believe it was an event of destiny; the pearl fell off the band. I thought to myself;

"What a perfect excuse to go to Tomas' store!"

I entered with the ring and sadly informed him

"Look, the pearl has fallen from the ring. Do you think you can fix it?"

He responded with a grin,

"Yes, of course, we can fix it. We have jewelers in Havana that fix all things. Give me the ring and I will travel to the jewelry store in Havana for you, and bring it back."

He did everything he said. Like a promise kept. I was fascinated with my new friend and happy with life, but how could I justify my visits to the store after he fixed the ring? A plan came to me overnight, I would loosen the pearl from the ring in order to visit Tomas for him to fix it, as an excuse to spend time chatting. I don't remember how many times I destroyed the ring for him to re-fix it (I wonder what he thought). I would hit the pearl in hopes it would fall off, and I would immediately go to the store to have him fix it again and again. Thinking back, I wonder if he realized what I was doing. Through time, our conversations grew more intense. He would sing me songs I'd never heard of while sitting in his small office smoking a cigarette. I remember his favorite brand was Salem. One day he said,

"I'm going to sing you a song."

He had a beautiful voice and sang quite lovely. He sang

"Contigo en La Distancia" (With you in the Distance)

It never crossed my mind he was grooming me for some unnatural cause, as he was only ever courteous and kind. I believe the absence of parental love led me to this moment.

During one of those fascinating days, he attempted to kiss me, but the look of confusion in my eyes must have swayed him to stop. I was left terrified and confused; several thoughts raced through my head, but the one that left me in shame was, *did I cause this to happen?* Tears streamed down my red cheeks. What a terrible thing, the shame kept me for quite some time from returning to the store, from returning to Tomas. I tried to understand what had happened because I knew I liked Carlos and didn't want anyone else. At the time, my appeal for Carlos was special, not certain if it was true, but it was a deep connection. I cared for him immensely; he was a wonderful, kind boyfriend, a respectable man who cared for me dearly; he was a true gentleman, attentive with wholesome morals. Carlos lived to give me anything I wanted; if I wanted a flying bird, he would get me the flying bird. He never did anything bad or harmed me in any way; he always did the right thing. It hurt me deeply to be in this extremely awkward and stressful situation at my age, which I had no way of handling. My trauma was leading the way.

To retell the story of Tomas pains me somewhat, although he never crossed the line after that, it left me questioning how I felt about him. I wondered if it was infatuation, or the love of the attention I received from him that made me feel special, or if he was, maybe, a paternal figure, which was something I lacked in my life. All these questions and yet only one I knew the answer to: did I enjoy my time with him?

The Crush Escapes

Months later, I began concentrating on my wedding to Carlos, who had finally, with a little loving push from me, proposed. One day, I had to travel to Havana to have my wedding dress fitted. On the way, I decided to drop by Tomas' shop to drop off the ring one last time and sit and speak with him before my wedding as one final goodbye to a treasured friend. Before I left the store, he expressed the urgency of me picking up the ring on Saturday, *not* Sunday. I found this strange and felt he was agitated, but I didn't focus on it. I had other matters on my mind: like my wedding. He proceeded to inquire what day I was to return from Havana, and I responded by confirming Saturday; he pleaded for me to be there; again, I thought nothing of it. When I returned from Havana on Saturday, I thought I would get to the shop in the morning, or at least midday. Still, the trip from Havana to Pinar del Rio, which normally took three hours, unfortunately, at that time, there was a particular movement going on in the island, wherein the communist party was moving the missiles from one side of the island to another. The packed bus I was riding in was detained and moved to the side of the road to let a parade of huge army trucks covered with tarps pass by. We were all curious about what the occasion was. All those huge, loud trucks drove past the main road, causing the rest of the cars to stop. It turned out that the trip, which, again, would normally take three hours, took six to seven hours. Needless to say, I arrived in Pinar del Rio after 5:00 pm, and by then, Tomas' store had closed. I didn't give it much importance and thought to myself,

"Oh well, on Monday, I will go and pick up the ring."

When Monday rolled around, I walked to the shop, but to my surprise, I didn't find him there. Thinking it was too early, I kept walking towards the other stores on the main street, which were located a few blocks down where a girl friend of mine worked. When I arrived at that store, I noticed the employees gathered around gossiping about something, and I asked what was happening. My friend said that the military had just seized his store. I was shocked,

"What do you mean they seized his store?"

She blurted,

"Yes, apparently the owner fled the island."

I screamed…

"No, this can't be!"

I frantically ran towards my treasured little shop, only to arrive and find a few employees confused, with nowhere to find Tomas. They recognized me perfectly well, based on the million times I visited the store with that silly little pearl ring. They even designated a name for me,

"The Girl with the Pearl Ring"

I frantically asked one of the employees,

"Where is Tomas?"

She, knowingly, blurted in the chaos,

"Don't act dumb, you know Tomas is not here."

Not understanding, I pressured her,

"What do you mean, don't be dumb? Where is he?"

She callously explained,

"Tomas abandoned Cuba and now this store belongs to the government."

In doubt and disbelief, I needed to know the truth,

"How is it possible that he is not here?"

I failed to comprehend, or maybe I just couldn't wrap the thought around my young mind that he would vanish without giving me at least an indication or sharing with me that this would happen. What did I do wrong? I thought we were *friends*. In total confusion, I asked her.

"Can you please search for my pearl ring? It might be in one of his drawers in the back office. Tomas asked me to pick it up on Saturday."

She curtly replied,

"No, I can't return the ring to you. Like I said, this store belongs to the government now."

When Fidel took power, he seized all the stores and homes that were owned by non-communist thinkers. The Communist Party had arrived, and I had no clue what was going on.

Walking back seemed like an eternity, leaving a river of tears etched in my path towards home. When my mother saw me enter in such a state, she calmly inquired,

"What is happening?"

I told her, between spurts of tears, snot, and spit,

"Mommy, Tomas left Cuba!"

The reaction from my mother was callous and expected…

"Oh well, don't expect a wedding gift from him now."

I felt the surge of all the pain, shame, and anguish that he would actually disappear without a warning, leaving me with nothing but more questions —always the questions! All I could do was recount in my head, every moment, every interaction, to find an indication that this was coming. The only thing that came to mind was when he sang to me, *"Contigo en la Distancia"* that last time we were together. I convinced myself that maybe with that song, he was trying to tell me that he was leaving. *Was that his way of telling me?* In those days, certain things were rarely spoken, because if you said the wrong thing to someone, it could put escape plans in jeopardy. There were spies everywhere now in Cuba, and you didn't know who to trust. Tomas' escape from Cuba left me with a horribly immense sadness.

A familiar feeling visited me — a whisper that leaned ever so close: *you have been abandoned again.*

The Wedding Bells Came Ringing

Antonio, Carlos, Me, Lucia

A few months after Tomas left, I finally completed all the preparations to marry Carlos; everything was ready. I once heard an old saying: "If your wedding starts badly, your marriage will last for years." — *Don't let that fool you.* We planned our wedding day during a tremulous time in Cuba when it was experiencing the globally debated missile crisis, which left the island in turmoil, grief, and confusion; we married on November 4, 1962. The Cuban people, including us, didn't have anything; there wasn't any gas or food on the island. Carlos and I were due to be married at 4:00 pm in the Cathedral "*Pinar del Rio,*" a small, quaint little white church with a tall, triangle bell tower, stone pillars that reached the sky.

Immediately after us, another couple (Joe and Tracy) were set for 4:30 pm. The couple was a close friend of ours and a colleague of Carlos. We made plans with Joe and Tracy to leave together after our vows to our honeymoons. We decided to drive in a car, which was borrowed from a friend, for our honeymoon trip to Havana. As it turned out, we were unable to because there was no gasoline available anywhere. The only gas available was for the government officials, and since we did not belong to the government, there was no way to obtain gas for our trip.

Cathedral Pinar del Río

I arrived at the church ready to get married a little after 4:00 pm. When the wedding march began to play, I positioned myself to walk down the aisle when I casually looked over to the altar and noticed the wedding party frantically trying to signal me to stop and go back, and then, to my surprise, I noticed Carlos was not standing at the altar. The music suddenly stopped as I rushed back outside when a guest shared with me that Carlos had not arrived at the church. I desperately asked,

"What do you mean Carlos has not arrived?"

He repeated in disbelief as well,

"No, Carlos has not arrived."

In Cuba, not every home had a telephone or a way to contact anyone, let alone Carlos, to find out what was happening. There I was, standing outside the church by the tall white stone pillars, frantically crying in my homemade satin white wedding dress, hoping he didn't abandon me. I believed most of the attendees might have thought I was crying because Carlos had changed his mind, but in reality, that was not why I was hysterically crying. I knew deep in my heart that Carlos was not going to leave me stranded at the altar. I was in fear that the delay was a sign from God sending me a message that the marriage was not meant to be. The couple was scheduled to get married after we had arrived. When they reached me, standing outside crying, they curiously asked,

"What happened?"

Someone explained to them that my groom had not arrived. The couple decided to get married first in order for the priest not to close the church and give Carlos enough time to arrive.

Carlos finally arrived with his mother, who was an angel loved by everyone. It turned out since Carlos lived in a neighborhood outside of the city, the only way to the church was through La Carretera Central, which was the main road that went from one extreme side of the island to the other, he ran into the famous Russian caravans that were transporting the missiles through the street at the same time causing every car to stop and wait for the military caravan to pass, making Carlos late for our wedding; it wasn't my sins that stopped the wedding, it was Fidel Castro.

All Things Have An Expiration

Me, Carli and Kelly

Carlos is a spectacular man, a man who gave me the greatest gift in life: my two beloved children. He was a wonderful husband who loved me dearly, and I believe he still does today, as a dear family member would forever. I regret not being able to love him as he loved me, but the heart is not an object to be controlled; instead, it is a muscle that needs room to throb and knows not what the mind yearns for. The youth can't conceive the intricate fibers of love. I had faith that Carlos was the man God intended for me, not just to love and have a family, but to escape my situation and a life of loneliness in Cuba. However, I shortly realized the escape would be temporary since my exit from the island would be extremely delayed. I was unable to leave as quickly as I had imagined or wanted to. Life continued, and a year later, one day, I became pregnant with my first child, Carlitos, a smart little blonde joy of a son. Apparently, with no way of getting birth control (as they were not available in Cuba), two years later, I had my second child, Kelly, a precious little girl who smiled with her eyes, all the while waiting to flee. The exit from Cuba wouldn't come for several years.

Carlos, Carlitos, Kelly and Me

The marriage flourished for seven years, although in reality, we never owned our own home. After our wedding, we moved in with his mother, siblings, and aunt. They were generous, but we had a room with no privacy. I was a sixteen-year-old spoiled brat who had no real example of a loving family, so having a family of my own? Insanity! Within that household, I eagerly awaited for my freedom while living with them for a period of five years. His family was truly gracious and I have nothing but good things to share about them, falling in love every day with the tender togetherness.

One day, after a small altercation with someone in my family, I went to live with my mother. In a childish manner, I proposed to Carlos an ultimatum: leave with me or stay here. Like the good and honorable man he was, he followed me. We began living with my mother, who situated us in a small room where the four of us would sleep. At that time, the kids were around four and six years old. Immediately, Carlos was designated to work in the infamous cane fields; in Cuba, those who wanted to leave the country would be sent to work in the fields as punishment. Unfortunately, Carlos was at the ripe age of military recruitment (men in military recruitment could not leave Cuba until the age of 27), and he was obligated to work in the fields. The labor for the men who were forced to work in the cane fields was strenuous and hard.

The time came when I faced the painful decision to leave my marriage. I knew my love for Carlos wasn't the same love he held for me. It wasn't fair for him to keep being married to a woman who didn't share his deep, eternal feelings. I, longed for myself to find true love within us, but while his love was burning, mine grew colder with each passing day. I was cracked porcelain, and couldn't find my own glue. One day, as the time grew closer for me to leave Cuba, he returned from working in the cane fields, his body dripping with sweat, his hands swollen and worn from the cutting of the cane, I cold-heartedly sat at the border of our bed and began,

"Carlos, I want a divorce."

The words left my mouth unceremoniously. I felt faint before I realized I was holding my breath.

He was confused, and his look broke my heart. His tone was somber.

"Why, Clara?"

I heard him whisper as if his life force was torn out from within him. I tried to be as honest as I could be without further hurting him,

"I'm no longer in love with you, the way you are with me."

I felt the weight of the pain I had just served him, expecting an outburst, a scream, terrible words... but none came from him. Instead, he handled his worst fear like a true gentleman. He was left speechless for what I felt was 30 minutes when his voice broke the silence.

"The only thing I ask is to never be separated from my kids. When you leave Cuba, don't leave me here, take me with you."

Staring into his pleading eyes, I whispered,

"Carlos, that will never happen. You're their father and will always be near them."

The one thing I would never do is let my kids go through what I went through to live a life unloved. This was one of the first drastic decisions that slowly began to mold my life and change it forever. And it broke us all. Each of our porcelain fragments collecting on the ground.

Carlos was always close to the kids, although, in the beginning, there was an enormous amount of sorrow toward me. It burdened me greatly, thinking of the heartache I caused him and his family, whom I adored. He never deserved it, but in the end, it was either his happiness or mine. *This island eventually carves a survivor out of you.* I was also quite young, being only 23 years old, with the rest of my life ahead of me. I don't believe family and people around us knew that it was one of the most challenging decisions I had to make in my life. Instead, I'm pretty sure they blamed me for ruining Carlos' life. I wished they knew how long and hard I thought about it, envisioned every scenario, and hoped for a different outcome, but once I decided, I did it knowing it was for the best for both of us. It's difficult to express, but I was utterly selfish at the root of that decision, not exactly thinking about Carlos or the kids. *Does this make me a monster? Or does it make me human?* I think it made me want to choose life, to choose hope, to choose freedom. It's like you're on a boat and one oar is happiness and the other is sacrifice, and you need them both to cross the water.

It seems when one is young, one is selfish, but always true to their hearts. After a couple of months, I found a lawyer and commenced with the divorce. The divorce was exhausting, but what ensued was painstakingly tense. The entire family blamed me, was against me, and spoke horrible things about me, ultimately branding me the wicked one. They made me feel as if I were evil, never understanding why I would ever divorce Carlos. I couldn't believe the thought that not one person understood that it could be possible for the decision I made to be a good one for both of us in the long run. I, like most of us, didn't care what others thought or what others believed me to be. I knew in my heart who I was and what I wanted, and no one could take that away from me, that I could control.

Before I left Cuba, Carlos' father, Candido (a serious, highly respected man), who was serving life in jail for being a Lieutenant in the Batista regime, was scheduled to be sentenced to death by the Castro regime via firing squad. I remember most of Carlos' brothers were also in jail at one point. The youngest, Al, who was about 17, tried to escape from jail, but as he climbed over the fence for his freedom, he fell and broke both legs. Carlos was also being tortured in jail as well at one point. It took for one of Candido's son who was not in jail to reach out to someone higher in power to grant him clemency. Candido was ultimately jailed for 20 years before the United States government freed him as a political prisoner to bring him to the United States. Candido lived in the United States with all his children until he was 105 years old. At one point, Carlos ended up being imprisoned over five times, and each time, they would take him out, line him up the wall and pretend to shoot him. *This island eventually carves a survivor out of you.*

Finally, Goodbye Cuba

Carlitos and Kelly

Several months later, finally, the day had arrived when I was set to leave Cuba. The day was November 19, 1970. I never thought that day would ever come. I exited Cuba at 24 years old, with a seven-year-old boy and a five-year-old little girl, to an unknown new world with only the clothing on our backs and no understanding of the English language. The Cuban military stripped every item we held dear to us on the tarmac before entering the airplane. They even stripped my kids of their possessions and jewelry; the Cuban government held nothing back and cared for no one, not even kids. But secretly, I was happy to leave.

We were afraid for our lives, as they treated us maliciously till the very end. Deserting Cuba was a horribly difficult decision. I loved my country, but communism flourished, and I dreamed of freedom for my kids and myself. I refused to have

44

my children go hungry any longer and live under a communist regime, where there was a lack of the bare living essentials, or live in fear of the military taking my children away for service to the communist army. The lack of food spread across the island, wherein the government would give every household a card for their portion of groceries. A family, no matter what size, would get an allowance of one gallon of milk, two slices of meat, and two eggs to last you for a month for the entire family. People in Cuba were growing hungry by the day.

I had plans to live with my father, who was living in Puerto Rico with his new family at the time. I had not seen him since I was 11 years old. My father never had the chance to know me as an adult, having fled Cuba when I was a child. We were practically unknown to each other, yet I was depending on him to start my new life in the United States.

Well, Hello Gorgeous (Miami)

In those days, once you left Cuba, you could never return. It was a sudden exile. I didn't have time to actually sit down with my thoughts about leaving my beloved country, which entailed leaving it forever and never being able to see my family or friends ever again. With all those emotions to unpack, I had to deal with the fact that they would not allow me to take any personal items, any mementos to remind me of life here with those that I cherished.

My departure was set during the month of November, so naturally, thinking it was winter, I prepared my kids, as well as myself, to wear winter clothing. My blonde-haired, adorable little boy, Carlitos, had a wool suit, and my smiley face daughter, Kelly, wore a short pink velvet dress with long sleeves, leaving me with a red mini-skirt, which I handmade myself. I would sew all my kids' clothing and even cut their hair to save money. When we landed in Miami, the weather was horribly hot and humid, as it was in Cuba, but for some reason, I imagined that when we arrived in the United States, it was going to be cold. I haven't the faintest idea where that idea emerged from. Goes to show you how much Cubans really knew about the outside world. We arrived at the Miami Airport, scared and unfamiliar with everything and everyone around us, only to be scooted out like cattle to the house where they were holding all refugees arriving before being processed through immigration to allocate us in the United States. The majority of people arriving had someone from their families waiting for them. When we finally arrived, there was no one; no one was waiting for my disoriented kids or me. I remembered sending a telegram to my father from Cuba before I left, informing him of the day we were to arrive. I truly believed he would be there waiting for us. Apparently, the communist party had the last laugh because the person who sent the telegram at the postal office got the date wrong on purpose, so instead of me getting there on the 19th, they said I was arriving on the 20th. *Bastards!*

Having received the wrong flight information, my father flew from Puerto Rico to Miami to pick us up the next day.

La Casa de Libertad

My desperation went through the roof upon arriving at *"La Casa de Libertad"* (La Casa de la Libertad, also known as the Freedom Tower, which is famous for its role in receiving the Cubans who fled Cuba after 1959 in search of freedom. It was ultimately nicknamed *"El Ellis Island del Sur."*) and frantically scanning the crowded room of immigrants and families, only to see no one was there to pick us up. The anxiety and fear surging through my body was uncontrollable. Not knowing what I was going to do with my kids dressed in layers of clothing, probably boiling to death in that terrible heat, was terrifying. The look on my face must have indicated my desperation to the representatives at the center because they gave us our sandwiches, our first Coke, and whatever else to maintain us calm. There were huge rooms filled with dozens of small cots for those who had no place to go or who were traveling to other states for them to stay the night. I thought to myself,

"What am I to do?"

While frantically trying to figure out how to get out of that horrible place, I had just finished speaking with the attendant helping me communicate with Puerto Rico. They contacted me with Ela, my father's current wife, who explained that my father had flown to Miami the day before to wait for me because, supposedly, I was arriving the following day. He was staying at her mom's house; she shared her mother's telephone number so that I could contact my father and have him pick us up. During that process, my kids vanished — they went walking around to explore that huge room without me noticing, and they disappeared from my sight. When I finished talking to Ela, I darted out like a crazy chicken without her head attached to her body, looking all over that huge place for them. I was desperately at my wit's end when I exited onto a little playground where there were slides and swings and found them there, quite happy and content playing in the park (something they had never experienced). I grabbed them by their hands and contained my desperation while entering the pale room to request permission to call my father's mother-in-law to try to speak with someone who could gather us. I called the number they gave me, and nothing—no one answered the call. I commented to the woman letting me use the phone, who said,

"If you have the address to where he is staying, we can call you a taxi to take you there."

I was desperate to leave that place, so we took her up on her offer.

When the taxi arrived, we entered, but the taxi driver was American and only spoke English; meanwhile, I only spoke Spanish, so I just gave him the paper with the address, and he drove me there. When we arrived, as you know, I was penniless. I signaled him to wait, went up with my two kids, and knocked on the door of the apartment, where supposedly my father was, but there was no answer. When I knocked on the door, another door nearby opened. There was a kind lady who said,

"There is no one there. They went out."

She studied me for a moment—winter clothes and all…then asked,

"Can I help you with something?"

My voice spilled in desperation,

"Lady, I just arrived from Cuba, and my father was supposed to pick me up. I have a taxi downstairs who is waiting for me to pay him, but I don't have money. I don't know what to do."

The stranger looked at me and with a gentle voice motioned,

"Come inside to wait for him and I'll pay the taxi."

Thank God for good people in the world.

That first day in Miami was a psychological battle. Finally, after two or three hours of sitting in the neighbor's apartment waiting for my father, he arrived, surprised to see us. That night, he rented a room in a hotel on 8th Street, where we stayed, and the following day, we departed for Puerto Rico.

Life in Puerto Rico

Top from Left: Mariela, Eli, Me
Bottom Left to Right: Ela, Kelly, Elias, Carlitos

We arrived in Puerto Rico on a hot Saturday night. My father lived in an apartment by the beach with Ela, Eli, and Mariella, who were sweet teenagers by now. On Sunday morning, they took us to a beach club, which they were members, to socialize with their friends and spend the day enjoying the pool and swimming in the vast blue ocean. I loved the beach. One of my father's friends, who was his accountant, asked me,

"What do you do? What work did you do in Cuba?"

I answered reluctantly,

"I didn't work in Cuba."

Curious, he continued to inquire,

"Do you have any experience in office work or anything?"

I remarked quite proudly,

"I studied typing when I was young."

He shared that his friend, a business owner, was looking for a girl to work in his office. He extended an invitation for my father to bring me to an interview for the job. As I was eager to be independent and to start working, I immediately replied,

"Yes, of course, we will be there tomorrow."

On early Monday, we went to his office, and they hired me on the spot. I felt proud of myself, thinking that I had merely just arrived in a new country and I already secured a job. I worked there until about a year, after which I left Puerto Rico.

The business ended up being a company that manufactured water filters and bidets. It was a small family factory with around 5 employees. At the company, I distributed the work between the salesmen and those who would install the filters, as well as attending to the phones. After some time, and since I was bored having completed all my work, I began to sell filters over the phone for fun and to make the time fly by. I believed myself to be an overachiever and took pride in my work. Later, gaining momentum, I would add calls to the clients to collect the payments. At times, I would venture to the rear of the factory and help build the filters myself. The owners were quite kind to me and grew to care for me enormously: maybe it was all the decent work I was doing.

Father immediately enrolled my kids in a private school in *"El Condado"*. While I had no transportation, my dad would drive me to and from work every day, something I miss today. I earned $64 a week at that job, forcing me to take on other small jobs to make sufficient money to survive. (Hence, selling filters to get a commission.) My intention was to earn enough money to become independent and achieve some idea of happiness. I thought it would take a long time, but fortunately, or unfortunately, I don't know how to call it, it only lasted three months.

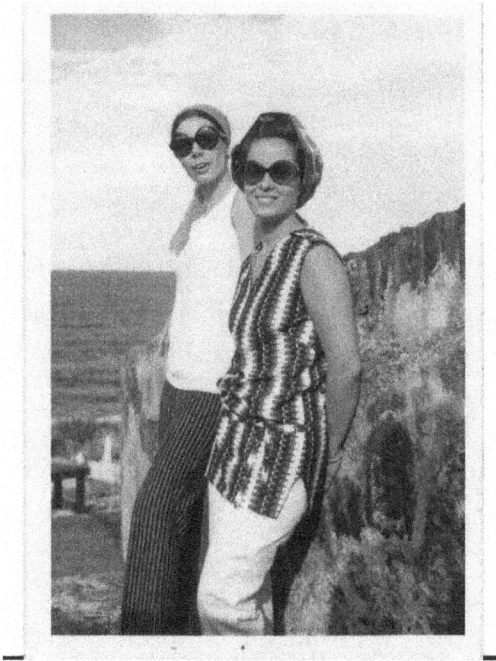

Normita (left) and I in Puerto Rico 1971

Normita, my childhood friend, who stood about 5'9" with beautifully thick, long black hair and an infectious smile, arrived in Chicago with Candito's family. Normita was Marta's sister, a loyal wife to Candito, whom I believe has earned her wings for being a godsend. Candito was Carlos' eldest brother, a boisterous, sweet man with slicked-back dark black hair who loved to boast about everything (he actually knew a lot about everything). Aside from Normita being my childhood friend, she was family. When she landed in Chicago, as soon as she had a chance, she contacted me in Puerto Rico. She shared with me that she wasn't happy living with Candito and Marta; nothing to do with her sister, just that she didn't align with Candito, which was not a big surprise, he was tough. She was eager to know if she could move to Puerto Rico with me, adding that Carlos had requested she help me with the kids because he heard I was struggling in Puerto Rico (Carlos was still in Cuba). When Normita asked if she could move to Puerto Rico, I happily said,

"Let me work on a plan. I'm currently living with my father and his family. We would have to move together and become independent women. Let me see what I can do."

In our excitement, all the while knowing but forgetting she didn't have any money and I didn't have any money to send to help buy the plane ticket. I reassured her,

"We will make plans to solidify you coming here."

I was living for almost three months in Puerto Rico, with the generous aid from my father, paying for the kids' school, all our expenses, clothing, etc., allowing me to save all the money I was making. I mustered the courage to speak with my father and shared with him of my plans to move out with Normita, asking for his financial help. To say that I was left in complete shock to learn that my father refused to help me move out on my own is an understatement. My whole life, every time I needed him, he was there to help me. I just assumed he would always be there for me. But in this particular matter, he was completely against it. I remember when I landed in Puerto Rico, he would make a point not to mention to anyone I was introduced to that I was divorced. In his mind, he was convinced that when Carlos would leave Cuba to join us, I would return to him and live a life with him and our kids. The idea that I was divorced with children in the 1970s was not satisfactory, to say the least. The idea of me moving in with Normita was even more unsatisfactory. As a matter of fact, he stated,

"If you want to do what you want, you will have to do it on your own account. I will not help you."

It was meaningless to ask for the money to buy Normita's plane ticket. My only option at that point was to speak with the owner of the water filter factory, my boss. I proposed to him a plan,

"I have a friend who has recently arrived from Cuba to Chicago who wants to live in Puerto Rico, but does not have money for the flight. Can you lend me the money, and as soon as she starts working, we can reimburse you?"

He politely asked,

"What does she do? It so happens that my brother-in-law, who owns a clothing factory, is looking for a secretary."

I continued to explain,

"She is a typist and knows how to work as a secretary."

He surprisingly agreed,

"OK, I'll lend you the money. When she gets here, tell her to go to an interview at the factory. I will speak with my brother-in-law, and when she starts working, she can pay me back."

What would I have done without good people? The funny thing is, Normita didn't know how to type. Sometimes, dire circumstances cause you to embark on crazy adventures. I was thrilled and shocked he agreed, but immediately called Normita to share the good news with the understanding that she would have to work for them as a secretary/typist until they were paid the ticket price. At that moment, Normita confessed to me, which I already knew,

"I've never sat in front of a typewriter."

I confidently said,

"Don't worry because you are going to sit in front of one as soon as you arrive in Puerto Rico."

He gave me the money, which I, in turn, sent to Normita for her to purchase a plane ticket to Puerto Rico. We were off!

The insane, funny thing about all this was: we had no idea where we were going to live. The next step was to speak with my father. I confronted him again,

"I know you don't want to help me with anything for my friend, but I will need you to help me find a place to live."

Needless to say, if you recall, I did not have a car, nor did I know how to really drive, although my dad did give me a few classes in a parking lot; I depended on him 100% for everything. He reluctantly said,

"Fine, I'll help you find a place to live, but after that, don't expect any more help from me."

I heard myself say. *"Ok, that's fine."*

On that day, we planned a drive with the family: Dad, Ela, her kids, my kids, and myself, much like we did every Sunday. During that particular trip, the four kids in the back seat became restless, and there was a small argument between them, which made me angry enough to punish them. Dad became enraged and immediately stopped the car on the street and pulled over, demanding everyone get out, so he could speak with me. Once everyone was out, he sternly requested that I sit in the front seat with him. While everyone was outside waiting, he said,

"This situation has become very uncomfortable. I want to know if you are still thinking of moving with your friend?"

I curtly answered,

"Yes, I'm still willing to move with my friend even though you won't help me. I have two arms, two legs, and a brain, and I think that is sufficient to be able to support myself."

His voice raised,

"I don't like the idea that you'll live with a woman because everyone will think you are a lesbian."

I lacked the knowledge at that age of such meaning and was left confused. Apparently, his fear was that people would find out I was living with a woman, and talk would spread throughout the world that we were partners. I was struck with anger, finding myself uncontrollably blurting out sharp, destructive words at him. He turned to face me and, with his entire being, slapped the words right off my mouth. This behavior was not new to me; I've gotten worse. With my face throbbing and tears streaming, I stood like a statue, stared into his icy, unemotional eyes, and whispered,

"This is the last time you hit me. Please, Dad, take me home, and tomorrow, help me find my own place to live, and you'll never have to slap me again."

That day I learned who my father truly was.

A week went by before he said,

"Let's go. I'm going to take you to see an apartment."

He brought me to a place where there was a small apartment with three rooms on one of the main streets in *"La Avenida Ponce de Leon."*

It was located at the top of a furniture store, where there were four little apartments in the rear and loud pounding from the floors; it was horrible, but I needed my space. The one we rented was small, with a tiny living room, dining room, and three pocket-sized bedrooms. He said;

"If you like it, let's go talk to the owner so you can rent it."

I didn't hesitate. The owner confirmed we could rent it, but he did not allow kids. My father assured him,

"No, she lives alone. She is waiting for her husband to come from Cuba. That's the reason why she needs the apartment now."

The owner responded,

"Ok, there seems to be no problem."

I believe my father knew the owner somehow, or they knew similar families. But whatever the case was he said,

"Let's rent her the apartment."

The rent was $90 a month. Luckily, the apartment was being rented fully furnished. My father handled all the paperwork, did whatever he had to do and assured us everything would be in place when I was ready to move.

After all the documents were signed and we left, my mind began to unravel; only recently had I fled from Cuba and its communist government, and all I could think of at the moment was,

"Oh, my God, what am I going to do with my kids when this man finds out I do have kids?"

My father assured me not to worry — the owner didn't live in that building and would only send a person one day a month to collect the rent. Suffice it to say, he never caught us. Goes to show you how desperate he was to get rid of me.

When I moved into the apartment, my father stopped helping me financially; now, I was solely responsible for paying the kids 'school, rent, food, and utilities; we couldn't afford a phone, so we lived without it. Since I also didn't own a car, I rode the bus everywhere, even to the laundry shop, with the kids' help. Those days were difficult, earning only $64 a week.

With the money I had previously saved while living at my dad's house, I was able to enroll in a class to learn how to drive. If I'm not wrong, I attended three or four classes only before I had the test. As a matter of fact, the only reason I think I passed was because, on the day of the driving test, I wore a blue mini skirt, causing me to distract the teacher. I'm ashamed to say I passed without even really knowing how to drive. I was learning the power of being a woman in America.

Ultimately, I was able to buy a White Toyota Corona, and thus began my life of driving. In the first few weeks, I was terrified, especially driving at night, as I had no clue how to turn on the headlights. One day, I begged a neighbor who worked at the gas station to lend me money for gas since I had none, promising to pay him back once I got paid. People were generous in those times. Being drastically broke, I couldn't even afford clothes. I remember getting Kelly a pair of second-hand shoes, which ultimately damaged her toes forever; the shoes were what we called *"cockroach killers"* because of the dangerously pointed tip design. I owned only one pair of shoes, which I wore every day for work, eventually breaking holes at the bottom of them and being unable to replace them. It was a stressful year, as I mentioned, sometimes I would have to go hungry, having no money to buy lunch, and forcing myself to drive home to eat crackers to last till dinner. I ate a *ton* of crackers. At dinner, I would give most of what we had to the kids.

Having no acquaintances or friends, only one couple in the same building would invite us to eat at their place because they knew we had no food. My decision to ultimately leave Puerto Rico was the best decision I could've made to attain an easier life for my kids and I; but if we stayed we would have never survived living the way we were.

The following months were even more difficult than the first. When it came time for groceries, there was only a $20-a-week allowance for food. We were drowning in despair and pining for possibilities.

The only person Normita knew was Adrian, an overly tanned smoker with giraffe teeth, who was married with two kids, and his family, who were from my neighborhood in Pinar del Rio. They lived roughly three blocks away from my mother's house in Cuba. In reality, I only knew him casually whenever he would scroll past our house. I somewhat knew the rest of his family including Lucas, his son, who would occasionally visit him. Adrian left Cuba via Spain, I believe, a year before I did. When we lived in Cuba, I was divorced from Carlos but still waiting for my exit papers, and Adrian was married and had Lucas and his daughter, whom I eventually was able to meet. I opened a business baking cakes with his sister, Taryn, a loud and sneaky lesbian (which I didn't know at the time), to support myself since the knitting was not enough. When I left Cuba, Adrian's family secretly handed me a sealed letter and a gold ring with the initials *"CCS"* to give to Adrian, which informed him that his family was good. This was a custom at the time, since the mail between Cuba and the United States was extremely limited and controlled, causing people to communicate with their relatives through the people who were leaving Cuba. Sadly, the militant government officers in Cuba stripped the ring from my finger but left me with his letter. *I've wondered how the lives of those evil Cuban militants ended up…hopefully, justice was served.*

Normita's family lived on the same block in Cuba as Adrian and were close to his family for some time. When Normita arrived in Chicago, she contacted him, and they reunited, and by this time, Lucas was already living with Adrian. Adrian helped Normita get established by running errands with her. She mentioned me to Adrian and how she was planning to move to Puerto Rico to help me with the kids. In November of 1971,

Normita invited Adrian to come to Puerto Rico for Thanksgiving, and he agreed. He stayed at our apartment for the weekend, and seeing how dire our situation was, he told us that it would be much better if we moved to Chicago. He mentioned to us that we could receive welfare there and be closer to family; he would also help us get a job to establish ourselves. Through time, we grew attracted to each other. He then left, and a few days later, we decided to move to Chicago—another life changing decision which veered my life into uncertainty.

The Windy City

Normita, Me, Kelly and Carlitos leaving Puerto Rico

We arrived in Chicago the second week of December 1971. It was already extremely cold, and we didn't come prepared for the winter; Puerto Rico lacked winters. The irony of this situation was that when we landed in Miami we were dressed winter-ready, yet when we landed in Chicago, we were not.

Immediately, when we arrived, Adrian picked us up at the airport. There waiting was Yayi, Carlos' little sister, who was living in Chicago with Cuca; Candito, a jokester man, with wife Marta (the saint), Gallego, Carlos' brother with his wife, Norma, a funny woman with an obscene love of food, all present at the airport. When we arrived, we were quite happy to see them as we had not seen them since we fled Cuba, yet here we all were reconnecting in a strange land. It was something quite special, really. We were all exiled, we were all out of the country we loved, and finding the family was something wonderful. The cousins became extremely energized, as well as my kids, now that they were all together. At that time, they shared with me the news that Carlos had arrived, but sadly, he was not

62

at the airport due to being admitted to the hospital, as he arrived somewhat sick. I was worried about him and hoped he would get better.

From the airport, I don't quite remember if we went to Adrian's apartment, but I do remember that Adrian was waiting for Kelly with a doll that was twice her size. I remembered thinking to myself that was a pleasant gesture on his part, even though Kelly didn't appreciate it at that time, only wanting her father and not a stranger, but I did give it some value, maybe trying to convince myself he was a good fit. We continued to the hospital to see Carlos, and the encounter with him and his children at the hospital was devastatingly emotional. It broke my heart. He had liver and stomach issues, although I often thought it had a lot to do with his stress; he tends to keep things inside. Gallego (my favorite of Carlos' brothers), who was at the hospital with us, asked me if he could take the kids home with him so they could stay a couple of days with their cousins. It was a win-win—the kids were eager to be with their cousins, and I desperately needed time to get myself settled in what was to be my new life. We were moving into a two-bedroom apartment where Adrian lived alone and we needed to accommodate four more people. The kids left with Gallego, and Norma and I left with Normita and Adrian to his apartment to commence the move.

The next day, early morning, I received a call from Gallego, who seemed quite distressed.

"Clara, I have to tell you something, but please don't get scared. I'm at the hospital with Carlitos; he tried to jump off stairs onto a tree and fell, breaking his arm."

You can already imagine the impact that signified to me at that moment, being terrified for my son and feeling hopeless with no insurance. They headed towards the same hospital where Carlos was admitted — what were the chances? The

63

doctor mended Carlitos' arm and he was settled in a room to stay overnight. All this seemed different from how they would do it in Cuba. In Cuba, usually, when an arm is broken, they straighten it, slap a cast on, and send you home. In this hospital, they didn't even allow me to stay the night with my son. Worried Carlitos would be scared and lonely with no way to communicate, as he didn't understand English, only Spanish; I walked over to Carlos' room, where he was still admitted and shared with him,

"Carlitos needs to stay the night, but they won't allow me to stay. Can you check on him?"

Knowing our poor little boy was traumatized, Carlos checked on him all night. The next day, they released him, and he was all the wiser with a white cast on his arm, which he wore proudly for a month, sharing the tale of how courageous he was.

The coming morning, we immediately went to the welfare offices to apply for aide. When I received my approval, I was more at ease. *Baby steps to freedom*, I thought. Adrian drove us to a nearby Catholic church where they distributed clothing to the community and also helped those who had recently arrived from Cuba. They generously gifted us winter coats. In the building where Adrian lived was an apartment with one bedroom that was for rent. I rented the apartment with the help from welfare. *Baby steps to freedom.* With excitement, Normita, the kids, and I immediately moved into our new apartment. Normita and I slept in the room, and the kids were on the sofa bed. Things were challenging, but getting better. Baby steps to freedom. Baby steps to happiness.

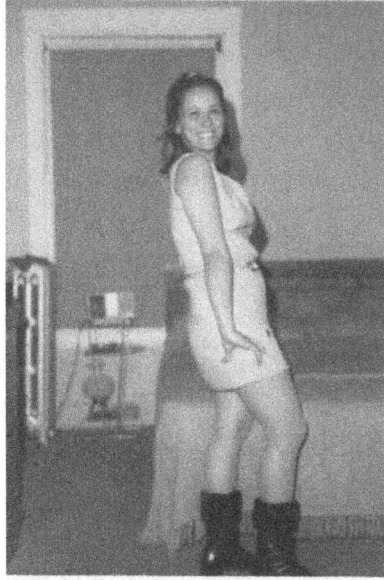

Me with my first pair of boots

Normita and I in Chicago

Once we settled into our new little, quaint one-bedroom apartment, almost three days later, we were eagerly preparing for our new jobs. I don't quite recall who connected us with that opportunity, but both Normita and I started working at a small box factory making boxes. On the first few days, Adrian drove us, since it was on the way to his factory job. Once I finally learned the route, he lent me the car, and I would drop him off at his work. Normita and I would then head to our jobs, and when we would finish our shift, since we left earlier, we would pick up Adrian. This was my life now: again being driven around by a man, trying to control my every action.

Winter slid in with the first snowfall (and to my horror), making it the first time I would drive in the snow. I had another distressing experience when I drove Adrian's old car that would stall at every other intersection. I still have PTSD with cars. Those were difficult times, but we overcame them again. I would repeat to myself:

God doesn't give you more than you can handle.

After about three to four months of living in that suffocating little apartment, we would cook dinners together, and Adrian would visit with his son, Lucas. Adrian was the person who drove us everywhere and resolved all our problems. He helped, which was an incredible support at the time, and he was desperately in need. My daughter might not be able to understand why I was with him, but necessity sometimes obligates you to make rash decisions and take opportunities as they come to survive; I believe we are all down deep inside the same. I was 24, with two small children, in a new environment, not knowing the language, and without family or friends other than Normita. The only thing I could do was cling to Adrian's help like a harness. He was a good provider, and I was working towards my future. What could go wrong?

Eventually, I left the box factory job a few months later. They treated me poorly. My heart breaks for factory workers. One day, I completely lost my temper at the boss for not allowing me a bathroom break. I pulled off the uniform, which they had provided, threw it on the floor, and shouted,

"I'll never work here again! I'm leaving."

I left and realized I still needed to wait for Normita so I sat in the bathroom and waited till our shift was over to talk about a grand exit. When she saw me, I exclaimed,

"I quit."

She looked at me in shock,

"Are you crazy Clara?"

I assured her,

"I'll never work in a place that treats me like an animal."

When I arrived home, I shared the story with Adrian, and he said,

"Let me try to get you a job at the factory where I work."

Men always pride themselves as being fixers. He spoke with the supervisor, who said there was an opening-(*sometimes they can help*)

"Bring her so she can get interviewed."

I still did not speak a bit of English, only maybe knew

"Yes," "ok," "please," and *"Thank you."*

But that was not going to stop me from moving to a better job. That factory was *"Wilson Sporting Goods"*.

I was employed at Wilson for several years in their football department, sewing shoulder pads, when one day, I was promoted to the golf club department. There, I worked piecework, which meant I earned money for each piece I produced. It required you to be standing the entire day in front of big drills and handing boxes full of iron heads for the golf clubs. I became productive quite fast and earned sufficient money to purchase our first home. *I will share that story further along in the book; (it's a long one.)*

Within the year, while I was working at the Wilson factory, we decided to move to a larger apartment. I rented an apartment with Normita, Adrian, Lucas, and my kids. Adrian and Lucas lived in the front portion of the house, which had a room and a balcony. Normita had her room, I had a room, and the kids had their room. That is how life began together. Little by little, Adrian and I grew to have a relationship because the reality was that I didn't know anybody else, I didn't socialize, and life was work, kids, and home. He must have known this and wanted to keep it that way. Shortly after we settled, our lives continued their course. Adrian and I became a couple, and after moving two more times, always on the same street, I finally bought my first car — a 1974 Brown Regal Buick. Eventually, Normita moved out and went to live with her sister again. Shortly thereafter, she met her future husband, Gil, a happy, boisterous, Southern, robust man, at the factory we worked at. During our time together, she met Gil, married him, got pregnant, moved to Alabama, had a beautiful daughter, Tracey, who went to have her own lovely kids and make Normita and Gil grandparents, where they lived happily ever after together until the day God separated them and sent them off to heaven. He went first, and then a couple of years later, she followed, having succumbed to cancer. I'll always think fondly of my best friend and all the wonderful times we shared. I wonder if she knows how much she helped me during those days living together, and I wonder if I helped her too. I miss my friend.

Eventually, Adrian and I married at everyone's surprise and dismay, especially my children. I try to think of those days with fondness, never forgetting the darkest times that came with the good.

The Infatuation Returns

It has been over 15 years since I last saw Tomas. One day, when I was living in Chicago, I married Adrian, my second husband, and our paths crossed once more. Adrian and I had traveled to Miami for my brother's wedding. On the same day as the wedding, there was the annual Pinar del Rio Reunion, where everyone who lived in Pinar del Rio (my hometown in Cuba) gathered to meet and celebrate freedom. This event happens every year, and everyone looks forward to seeing old friends who have migrated to Miami from Cuba. My intention was never to go to the Pinar del Rio Reunion Party. I was only mainly there for my brother's wedding. But as it turned out, one of our friends had already purchased tickets for us and we eventually attended the party after the wedding finished. At that point, I was genuinely excited to see old Cuban friends. God works in mysterious ways.

At the party, while sitting at our table, which was directly in view of the main entrance, we were casually in conversation with some old friend, when my sight caught a glimpse of what I was sure to be Tomas. I was left in disbelief. He glided in slow motion, entering the room with a stunning and elegant blonde woman. I was frozen. As if some great force was holding me in place. The last thing I ever imagined was to be reunited with the man who carried such a profound role in my childhood. They casually found their table and, like royalty, sat down. All I was able to do was follow their every move with my eyes, like a predator stalking its prey. My stomach started echoing like a marching band rally at a game that we were losing, and my hands were turning blue; was I suffering a heart attack, a panic attack… or was I merely in shock. After slowly gaining my composure with soft, steady breaths and making sure no one saw my paradigm shift, I made a beeline to the bar.

Not to grab a drink, which I desperately did need. Instead, I strategically positioned myself in a spot by the bar to wait for him. After several minutes, which seemed like hours, and no Tomas, I couldn't keep standing there like a mannequin on a window front. I formed a plan in my head to return to my table by walking past his table in hopes he would see me. The moment I arrived at his table, something stopped me, and ever so lightly, I saw myself tapping his shoulder. I didn't know what to expect. When he turned to see who was taping him and saw me, he leaped out of his chair, like a grasshopper startled by a cat, stood as tall as he could, and, I'll never forget what he shouted,

"Clara, Clara, muchacha!"

He immediately hugged me and turned to introduce his beautiful wife,

"Look, she is Clara, the daughter of Lola, my friend from child-hood."

As to justify the bear hug and excitement upon seeing me again, I gathered.

There, he instantly started questioning me,

"Are you married? Is your family here with you?"

I nervously murmured,

"Yes, I'm married."

He instantly excused himself to his wife and the table, grabbed my hand, which had been warmed by his loving touch, and guided us as if we were heading to my table to greet my family. But, instead of walking towards the table, he lured me to the dance floor, held me in his strong arms, and began dancing with me. There, his questions continued. I can only assume he was truly interested in how I turned out. After all, we were close and dear to each other, never having the opportunity to say goodbye.

"*Did you get married to Carlos? Do you have any kids? Tell me.*"

I nervously answered him,

"*Yes, I married Carlos, had two kids, divorced Carlos, and married Adrian Cacas. I'm living in Chicago, just here visiting.*"

He was eager to know,

"*When are you leaving?*"

My hands grew sweaty,

"*In two or three days.*"

At that moment, he took out a card from his pocket, pleading,

"*Please, Clara, if you can call me before you leave, I need to talk to you.*"

I agreed, and we both returned to our tables as if nothing grand had happened, but indeed, something grand had happened. Tomas had returned to my life. A ghost turned to flesh.

Back at my table, I sat down, trying to find the reality of it all again, as I drank my rum and coke, or *Cuba Libre* as we Cubans like to call it. I noticed Adrian had been chatting up at different tables with people we hadn't seen in years. He didn't even notice how long I was gone and I was happy about that. We were staying in the Ramada Inn, which was located by 70th Avenue, and the kids were staying at Gallego's house with their cousins. It was only Adrian and I at the hotel. When we arrived at the room that night, I immediately rushed to the bathroom to fish out the card from my purse that Tomas had secretly given me, like a giddy teenage girl. He owned a tire company, and his number was on it. I went to sleep dreaming of our reencounter. Something unknown was brewing within me.

The next morning, Adrian left early, as he always did, to get breakfast or visit someone, or something or other, the point being, I didn't care. I *did* care that he would return later in the afternoon, which would allow me time to plan my day and reconnect with Tomas. I scrambled to get dressed, but picking an outfit took some time (a woman always needs to have the right outfit when reconnecting with an old potential flame), and I was nervous and on high alert. Once ready, I searched for his card, which I intentionally tucked away in my purse, looked at the address, and as I was standing in front of the hotel window, I glanced to my left, and there was Tomas 'shop. *What were the chances? Was this a sign?* I stayed standing motionless for what felt like eternity, in front of that unwashed window, staring at my reflection, when I finally saw him drive by in his car. I followed his every move as he arrived, parked, and entered the building. I allowed him time to get settled, all the while looking through my hotel room window, when I called him. I felt like a spy. He picked up the telephone, and I whispered,

"You have a mustard-colored shirt on. Right?"

And he shockingly responded,

"Muchacha, do you have a crystal ball?"

I giggled,

"No, but I just saw you enter your office."

He quickly inquired,

"What do you mean you just saw me come into my office?"

As I explained,

"Yes. Do you know where I am? I'm at the Ramada Inn right across the street."

He exclaimed,

"I cannot believe it! Can I see you?

I immediately blurted,

"Yes, you can see me. Give me 10 minutes and wait for me by the hotel pool."

When I arrived, he was already there, patiently waiting for me. Sitting like a king on his gold throne. We immediately started talking, remembering our days together in Cuba and curious about each other with a million questions. It was a magnetic rhythm, with butterflies dancing in my stomach to his tune. I reasoned my nervousness had something to do with the fact that I left him being a young girl and now, I was a woman. I was seeing him with fresh eyes, the eyes of a woman, instead of that young, impressionable, and naive girl in the past. Interestingly enough, those similar sweet feelings I held for him then arose again now, making me extremely emotional, feeling mesmerized listening to him speak. He expressed his hope not to become strangers again and requested I keep in contact.

"Clara, when you return to Chicago, make sure to keep in touch. And when you return to Miami, give me a call so we can see each other again."

He shared with me that he had remarried and had another son that his business was doing rather well; and I shared more or less what happened when I got married to Carlos, and we got up to date with our lives. Then we separated once more. We never spoke about his departure from Cuba and I wondered why. Were we both in different head spaces about our relationship or was it just too painful to revisit? I'll never know.

Daughter and Father Reunion

Me, Kelly and Elias in Chicago

Life in Chicago was also difficult; working all day at a factory, which consisted of strenuous 8-hour shifts, constantly standing, walking, lifting, bending, and running around. Once at home, I would prepare and cook a delicious Cuban meal for the entire family, take care of the kids and get ready for the next day, and also please Adrian; this would happen every day. I felt myself wilting — a rose bush of only thorns, working all day, cooking, cleaning, and attending to my family. I would have loved it if one day someone would cook sometimes for me, but that never happened. Add to that exhaustion trekking to the laundromat, since the apartment didn't have a washer or dryer, with everyone's dirty clothing, and spending hours doing everyone's laundry. Luckily, after we purchased the house, we finally were able to have our own washer and dryer allowing me the convenience of doing it at home. I was still only thorns. I remember thinking that women are the real heroes of the world. We can run a country without men, but we are still human and need a break once in a while, or even a helping hand in order to feel appreciated.

My social life, as I mentioned before, was quite limited. I didn't venture to any events or places, I simply visited close friends for dinner, or they would come to our house. It was an ordinary and dull life. Since leaving Cuba, I hadn't had an opportunity to *enjoy* life. In the seven or eight years I lived in Chicago, I remember only going once to the movies, once to a restaurant, which a friend invited us for my birthday, but for the most part, I focused on being...logical. All the responsibility at such a young age wears you down, but I had to plow through. There were no other options.

After Wilson moved to another state and laid off all the employees, I welcomed unemployment. For the first time in God knows how long, I was able to slow down and focus on myself. I enrolled in college and studied English and typewriting. My thoughts were to improve my situation and find my balance in life. While attending college, an opportunity presented itself to me to set up a business. It was actually my father's idea. By the way, it had been seven years since I last saw my father. After six years of living in Chicago, one day on Carlitos' birthday, my father called. I was taken aback and somewhat excited to hear his voice. He greeted me as if we had spoken just the day before (this made my heart smile). He asked me about Carlitos and said he wanted to wish him a happy birthday. I handed Carlitos the phone and he congratulated him. He shared he was in Miami at the time and had divorced Ela. He mentioned that he still lived in Puerto Rico, but that he was visiting Miami because one of his kids was getting married. It was Mariella's wedding, and he had arrived in Miami for the wedding. I asked him how long he was going to be there, and he said he was staying till December to celebrate Noche Buena (Christmas

Eve) with them. It then occurred to me to ask him to come to Chicago for New Year's Eve and celebrate with us so he could see his grandchildren. Surprisingly enough, he said *yes!* We were reunited in December of 1976. The joy I felt those days with him will always live in my heart.

During my father's visit to Chicago, I was midway through collecting unemployment from Wilson and attending college. He, as a matter of fact, asked me why I didn't get enthusiastic and plan a business strategy. He was always of the opinion that we should never work for anyone and that we all should have our own business. He always felt that the owners always benefited from our hard work. Needless to say, he implanted the seed in my brain. I mentioned to him I would entertain the idea and let the creative juices flow. I thought maybe a bookstore since I loved books and literature, but in Chicago, it was mostly English-speaking and not Spanish. I didn't hamper on that idea (yet it found roots ultimately). On that visit, he told me he was going to travel to Houston in a couple of months with his brother, my uncle Carlos (the uncle that lost his hair), who lived in Houston and thought of visiting and wanted to see if I would join him to get to know the city. I agreed. I was open to new opportunities, and the chance of visiting a different state intrigued me.

On the trip, he shared an idea that occurred to him: for me to establish a dry cleaner business. He noticed that there was tremendous movement in the dry-cleaning business in Houston. Although it ultimately didn't happen there, it did spark a fire in me to make it happen *somewhere.*

When I returned to Chicago, I started considering the idea more seriously. I did notice it was a business that wasn't extremely complicated to learn, and that, in reality, it did have tremendous movement *(Dad did good research).* I commenced searching and found a dry cleaner that was for sale, but in a neighborhood that didn't call for that service, and a bit far from where I lived. Coincidently, the owner was Cuban and gave me the opportunity to stay with her for a week and learn how the business ran. Unfortunately, it didn't work, because I didn't like the neighborhood (it was quite dangerous for a woman) or the distance from my home, but I did learn the business in that week. I thought, well, if I could do this in a place near my home, it would be ideal. The wheels started turning, and I again began searching for a location closer to home. To my benefit, I found one in front of the kids 'school; the kids had moved from public schools to a private Catholic one called, "Our Lady of Mercy", which was located on Kedzie Street, and there, across the street, we found a small storefront that was empty.

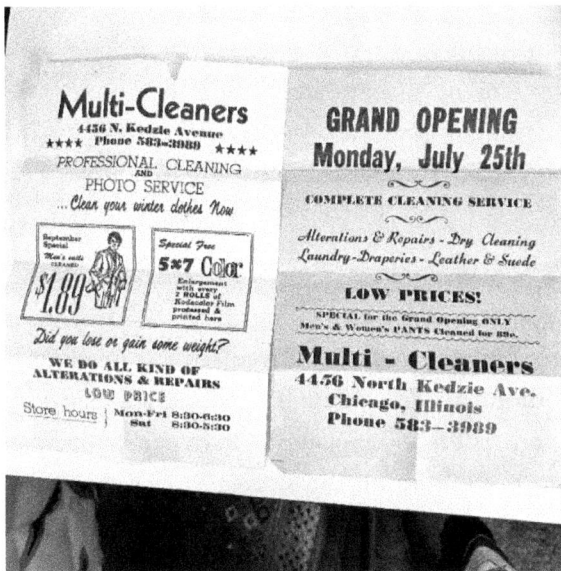

Multi Cleaners Grand Opening Flyer

Multi Cleaners

We had to build the counters, set up the racks, panel the walls, paint, and accommodate it to fit our business, but it was worth it. Although it was an enormous undertaking, in the end, it came out wonderful. I was on my way to living the American dream.

This new entrepreneur journey soon unfolded with me opening a full on dry cleaner's business. We cleaned and performed alterations on an industrial sewing machine I found, and in addition to dry cleaning services, I added film/photo development, sold clothing, and Adrian performed income tax services to customers on the side. The cleaners ran perfectly for a year until Adrian got laid off from The Wilson factory. It was then that he approached me with the idea of moving to Miami to find a better life. Chicago had become more difficult with the harsh winters and financial instability. The kids were older, and his son, Lucas, had already left to go study medicine in Santo Domingo. It helped make the decision to move from Chicago to Miami easier, knowing that Carlos' entire family was living in Miami (my father took it upon himself to free all of Carlos' family from Cuba-he saved the entire family, including Carlos). I spoke with the kids, and the decision was made. We were moving.

We found a realtor who helped me get a job at the insurance agency, Aetna, and listed the house and business on the market for sale. We were able to sell the dry cleaner quite fast, all the while working at Aetna. Those three months working there allowed me the experience to learn the insurance field, as my duty was to handle all the incoming claims via telephone. When summer came around, in August of 1978, we made the move towards Miami. I was confident we would have a happier life there. After all, I survived Chicago.

I failed to mention that when my father was visiting Chicago, he thought Adrian and I were married, but that wasn't the case—we were actually just living together. I neglected to explain to my father that I wasn't married. It just didn't feel right. The last thing I wanted was to deceive my father or upset him, so I immediately asked Adrian to marry me, which he did. It was not the best way to start a marriage, but in my mind, I wasn't sinning anymore, at least with this. This was the produce of being raised Catholic. Adrian and I decided to marry at the courthouse on December 4th due to my father's arrival at the end of the month, as I wanted to be legally married when he arrived. In hindsight, that decision would determine a harrowing future for me and my children. The only people who attended the reception were Yayi and Cuca, who have always been family to me. Marrying Adrian derailed my destiny and caused it to be a decision I would later regret.

Life in America

Me in front of our first home in Miami

In May 1978, I flew to Miami from Chicago in search of an apartment for us to move into. I believe my father was living there at the time. He supported me in finding a temporary apartment to stay in while I found a house to buy. We rented a tiny apartment in an area called "Sweetwater," which was adjacent to the famous "Tamiami Trail". I wanted the kids to have somewhere to stay while we got settled, but the apartment only had one bedroom. I remember the bed had wheels and would roll anytime someone would move (the kids would giggle every time). As it happened, the realtor who sold my house in Chicago recommended a realtor in Miami. I met with him and explained the parameters to find a house as fast as possible. I instantly fell in love with Miami, the people, the weather, and the food!

We allocated some temporary furniture in the apartment until the furniture arrived from Chicago to make it homely. The realtor, who wanted to help, inquired as to my occupation.

I explained that I had recently arrived from out of state and was unemployed.

He continued asking,

> *"Are you looking for work?"*

I jumped at the question,

> *"Yes, of course, I need to find a job as soon as possible."*

He continued,

> *"What did you do previously?"*

I proudly replied,

> *"I worked at an insurance office."*

He was pleased to hear and excitedly went on to explain that he had a friend who works for an insurance company that mentioned just yesterday how they were looking for someone and if I knew of anyone interested:

> *"If you want, I can put you in contact with her?"*

I felt aligned,

> *"Perfect! Of course, yes!"*

He shortly after connected me with the woman in charge, who was, by the way, quite divine. She informed me,

> *"Yes, we are looking for a girl to take claims via telephone."*

I was happy to share with her that I performed the same thing in Chicago, so I was indeed experienced in it. I further explained that having recently arrived from Chicago, I didn't own a car.

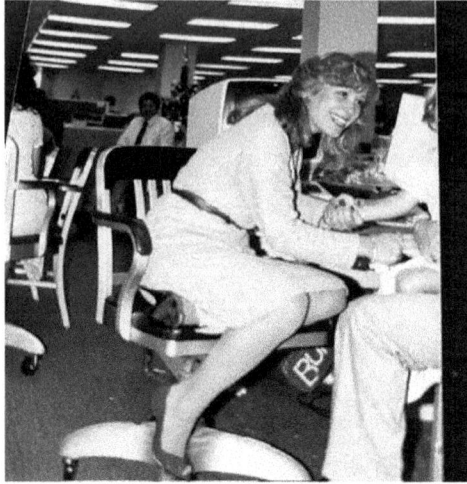

Me at The Travelers Insurance Co.

She assured me not to worry, then:

"Where do you live?"

When I responded, she took a moment before laying out my future,

"I live close. If you like, I can bring you tomorrow with me. As long as you arrange for someone to pick you up at the Travelers Insurance Company, I can take you. You can go with me to get interviewed. If they accept you, then it's perfect."

That is what we did. The following day, she picked me up and drove me to The Travelers. The head of personnel was a striking, green-eyed young woman, Mayra Perez, who was conducting the interviews. By this time in my life, I was certain I had angels guiding my every move, leading me to happiness and independence.

The interview was a typewriting test, of which I failed three times because my fingers were faster than my brain, causing me to make errors. *Dumb brain, come on, catch up with my fingers*, I thought. It seemed she was in dire need to fill the position because after the third failed attempt at the test, she said:

"Look, you don't need to rush, as this is not a speed test, it's an accuracy test. Therefore, please go at your own pace, slowly without errors, which is what I am interested in."

She gave me a fourth try, and I finally (barely) passed. It seemed she liked me and immediately offered me the job — my first job in Miami. I started working within the week. Shortly, Lucas had arrived with Kelly, Carlitos and our dog, Zombie (who eventually ran away from where he was left, which destroyed the kids), to await our new home. Finally having my car, I commenced my journey working at The Travelers. This decision solidified me to forge lifelong friendships.

I worked eight wonderful years at The Travelers and developed the friends that I have today. I began taking off all the auto claims and then was transferred to the worker's compensation department as an assistant to one of the claims adjusters. In that position, I was lucky enough to have a boss named *"Mr. Hallman"*, whom I dearly admired. Hallman was a tall, lanky man with gold rim glasses and a particular gap between his two front teeth. He saw the potential in me and said:

"Why don't you try to take the adjuster exam?"

I was in shock:

"No way, under no circumstances. I'm not prepared for that."

He affirmed:

"Yes, you can. I will help you."

In the meantime, I finally settled in my newly purchased house in *"Westchester"*. Westchester was a middle-class neighborhood where my children were raised through their teens. Two months later, Adrian arrived from Chicago to live with me and the kids. I must admit it was lovely not having Adrian around, when it was just me, Kelly and Carlitos. Lucas left for Santo Domingo to study medicine, and we started our new life in Miami. I felt everything was going to change for the better. When classes began in August, the kids attended school in Rockway Elementary, and we settled into our life until 1980 when the shit hit the fan, and the *"Mariel boat-lift"* began.

Returning to Cuba

Me ready to return to Cuba with tons of clothing on

Let me share a bit of history - In Cuba, when I left in 1970, there were no means of communication, no flights, and no visits. When one left Cuba, they left forever. The exits were permanent with no form of return unless the Fidel Regime fell, ended, and Cuba was free from its communist grip. Only then would we be able to return. Unfortunately, as we all know, this hasn't happened. When I left, there was no way of having contact with the family back in Cuba; in addition to no contact, the calls were extremely limited and barely impossible to make, being that there were no phones in the house. When I did want to call my family in Cuba, I would have to call a neighbor of theirs, and it was quite tricky to connect. Letters would take three to four months to arrive, therefore, communication with Cuba was practically non-existent. We had limited access to the world, if any.

Finally, in 1979, they opened limited flights, which they called "*Los Vuelos De La Comunidad*" or "*The Flights of the Community*".

A priest or a reverend to one of the churches in Hialeah thought to get together with the Cuban government and create some flights for the Cuban residents in the United States who had families in Cuba. Making it possible to visit through a third-party country; in this case, it was Jamaica. At that time, precisely, I received notice that my mother was having health issues. They found some irregularities in her heart, making her fragile and unwell. We thought that my return would not be prior to ten years, but unfortunately, I needed to return to Cuba to see my family, mainly my mother. All the while not knowing if she would survive or if I would ever see her again, or be able to leave. For days, my anxiety flared at the thought. I was one of the first people to return to Cuba shortly after they opened the first flights to there. I believe, out of our town, I was the first one to return from the United States. The reception that they gave me was one much like the welcoming of the Queen of England.

The Cuban regulations on what to take on your trip extremely limited the items you could bring. Therefore, everything I carried with me was with the intention of leaving it to my family. There was an incredibly ugly misery in Cuba which killed hope in the people. I packed as much clothing as I could stuff in the luggage, considering the limited weight constrict. In true criminal behavior and as a way of sticking it to the government and helping my family, I engineered a plan to put on as much clothing as I could. I dressed up with 5 underwear, 3 pants, 4 skirts, 3 bras, and so on. I looked like a Halloween character that weighed about 250 pounds. Needless to say, it was an intense trip. Our layover was in Jamaica, staying one night and the next morning flying to Havana; I was determined to see my mother one last time.

Top from Left: Me, and my step-brothers Jose & Tony
Bottom from Left: Lola, Antonia and Dulce

The reunion with my family after nine years was quite memorable, filled with various feelings and emotions. My mother, who was 56 at the time, was unable to travel to Havana and welcome me due to her health, so my brothers went in her stead. When I arrived at my childhood home in Pinar del Rio and saw my mother in her weakened state, my heart broke. The last time I saw her, she was a vibrant, strong, young woman, always very active, but what was before me was a weak old lady walking slowly, hunched over, and talking under her breath. That sight affected me immensely, and for a second, I found myself thinking, *Did I do this? Did my leaving Cuba kill my mother?*

I spent an emotional week in Pinar del Rio. I found out that a week before my arrival, my family did all they could to find food for my visit food, let me just say, that they didn't even have for themselves. This was their reality. They were able to trade with neighbors and work for meat and vegetables, and strived to do everything they could in order to make me comfortable and happy. Meanwhile, they were starving. They were kind-hearted, generous, and simple people. People in Cuba were in dire need of basic living essentials, in addition to food, clothes, and utilities. They were ecstatic with everything I carried to give them. During the communist regime, Cuba only had things for the communist party, but nothing for its people, who just wanted to be free. My family didn't have any idea of all the things you can have in the United States. When I opened the luggage and they saw gum, lipsticks, socks, and everything else, they thought it was truly a magical, marvelous miracle. Remember back when you were young and waiting for Santa Claus to leave all you ever wanted? That is how they must have felt, that pure joy. Everything was as if Santa Claus had arrived. That week was a bit contradictory, as it was delightful and heavy all at once. I took a walk through our neighborhood and saw all my old friends, the broken-down houses, destroyed roads, and people in misery. There was no toilet paper and no water at times; the electricity would go on and off as determined by the government. We were all being watched at all times. I was being followed every time I ventured out, walking through "*La Calle Real*", which, if you recall early in the book, I mentioned where all the stores were. My entire trip there was someone following me at all times. I feared for my life and for the life of my family. When the week in Cuba came to an end, I found myself eagerly ready to return home. My heart couldn't hold any more sorrow, and at that moment, a thought shifted my thinking, but was I selfish in thinking those thoughts? I felt truly blessed for everything I had at that moment. How could I ever complain again about my life, after witnessing the immense despair happening in my beloved land? That day, I learned to be forever grateful for my life and everything in it.

The government forced me to stay at *"The Hotel Nacional",* the night before returning to the United States. I believe they might have been spying on me till the end. My entire family accompanied me to the hotel. But first, I decided to take advantage of the last day and travel to visit my family, on my father's side, in Havana. At this time, my entire family was still living in Cuba: my uncles, cousins, parents, brothers, and sisters. The only person I had in the United States was my father. My family never had the urge to come to the United States, but when I spoke with them and shared my wish for them to think about it and try to, in some way, leave Cuba. My mother was reluctant and somewhat of a coward in experiencing new things, so it was no surprise when she said,

"No, I will never leave here. I am good here."

My brothers, cousins, and uncles, especially the younger generation, on the other hand, all wanted to leave and come to the United States. Unfortunately, at that time, there was no way or form for a resident to leave. My chest flooded in devastation for them and for us.

Upon my return, I remember perfectly the moment when I rapidly boarded the crowded bus, which was heading to the airport, turned to look out the mildew-stained window for one last look, and saw all my family waving goodbye, never forgetting their expressions. I had sadly expressed to them prior,

"I feel terrible about what I'm about to share, but I will never return to Cuba. The next time we will see each other will be in the United States. That is the only way we will ever see each other again because, in the state of how this country is, I will never return."

Effectively, that is how it went, as of now, I've yet to return to my beloved country.

Peruvian Embassy and El Mariel Incident

The boat we bought to travel to Cuba to free our families

Beginning in 1979, Cuban dissidents began to assault international embassies in Havana to demand asylum and hijacked Cuban boats to escape to the United States. The first such attack was on May 14, 1979, when 12 Cubans crashed a bus into the Venezuelan Embassy. Several similar actions were taken over the next year. Due to this uprise, Castro insisted that the US help Cuba prosecute the boat hijackers, but the US ignored the request.

On April 1, 1980, bus driver Hector and five other Cubans fervently and with purpose drove a bus into the gates of the Peruvian Embassy. Cuban guards started shooting. Chaos ensued, wherein two of the asylum seekers were injured and one guard was killed. Castro demanded the release of the exiles to the government, but the Peruvians sternly refused. Castro responded with a vengeful and calculated act on April 4th by removing guards from the Embassy and leaving it unprotected.

Within hours, over 10,000 Cubans stormed the Peruvian Embassy, demanding political asylum and freedom from communist Cuba. Castro agreed to allow the asylum seekers to leave.

In a surprise move (and a sneaky way of releasing criminals to the US), on April 20, 1980, Castro declared that anyone who sought to leave the island was free to do so, as long as they exited through the Mariel Harbor, 25 miles west of Havana. Within hours, desperate Cubans took to the cold waters, risking their lives to flee from a cruel and greedy government, only to wait for days for their relatives from South Florida to send boats to hopefully pick them up. Many died in the process.

The Mariel boat-lift ended by mutual agreement between the two governments in late October 1980. By then, as many as 125,000 Cubans had reached Florida. Some of the dead are unknown.

In April 1980, the Cuban government decided to open a port, which was called "*El Mariel*," dedicated to all the Cubans who wanted to exit the Island; with one caveat: they had to have someone pick them up in a boat at the Mariel. During that period, I lived in Miami, with all my family still living in Cuba. In reality, I was not sure if they even wanted to come to the United States because when I left Cuba, they were still unsure about leaving. Things changed when El Mariel was opened with everyone in Cuba wanting to leave at that point. I was fortunate enough to communicate with my family in Cuba via telephone, and once again, I asked them if they were capable and willing to abandon the island. If so, I would commission a boat and attempt to get them out. To my utter surprise, they said *yes*. Even my mother reluctantly said yes at the end. She realized if everyone was leaving, she had no choice but to leave with them. I didn't have a boat, and everyone who had a boat, a raft, or a dingy all took off to Cuba to pick up relatives. It was chaos at the ports and desperation on the waters.

It wasn't as easy as everyone thought it would be. Big surprise. Everyone thought they would arrive with their boats at the Cuban Mariel Port, and their families would miraculously be taken to them, and they would return to Miami with their families in tow. But, since our imagination is greater than reality, it was undoubtedly not like that at all. El Mariel lasted from April to October—seven devastating months. When July came around, I spoke with my father because the family I had in Havana (my uncles, aunts, and cousins), wanted to leave as well and thought he would help me. I asked my father to help me buy a boat to sail to Cuba and pick up all our family: my mother's family, my father's family, and, if possible, Adrian's family. Adrian also had all his family in Cuba— his daughter, ex-wife, mother, and brothers. *What was I thinking?*

Adrian and I decided to combine all of our savings to purchase the boat, with my father giving half the money we were able to buy it. Adrian, who had sailed with his cousin, German Sole, already had a boat ready to pick up their family. When German heard the news that El Mariel was open, he asked Adrian if he wanted to join him, so Adrian went. When they arrived at El Mariel, the Cuban government didn't release their families to them. Instead, they filled their boats with criminals, strangers, and none of his family members. The government never guaranteed to release your family to you. Instead, they would fill up your boat with anybody, preferably criminals. The government would first take out all the mentally insane patients from the asylum, they would take out the criminals from the jail, and force them on the boats that were there waiting for their own families to sail them to Miami. With that said, on Adrian's first trip, he was unable to get his family out of Cuba. We then decided to go forward with buying a boat in order for him to go back again alone and assure his procurement of his family. We paid a captain to navigate the boat. *Oh captain, my captain...*hell on earth.

The process with the Cuban government was chaotic at the pier. Once you arrived at El Mariel, you would present to the officials the list of the family members you wanted to claim. When Adrian went a second time, he lingered about six weeks at El Mariel waiting for them to give him our family. Sadly, again, they didn't give him any of our family members, and thus, shortly after, they closed El Mariel. He was forced to return to Miami with another boat full of strangers, criminals and mentally disturbed, as they evacuated all the boats at the pier and closed it. They told him they were closing and that it was finished, causing him to return again without the family we so desperately tried to free. I cannot imagine what I would have done, fighting waves, seasickness, and hunger for days with nothing to show for it.

When he returned to Miami after being away for so long, he lost his job. As you can imagine, besides being devastated for failing to free our families, he was frustrated at losing his only form of income. No one understood during the time he was waiting at El Mariel the immense pressure we felt and the intense time we endured simultaneously. This destroyed him, as ultimately it did me. Still, I was enamored by the thought of my family finally coming. I started preparing to see my mother, brother, cousins, and uncles. Logically, I knew once they arrived, they would all come to stay at my house until they could afford to live on their own.

After all the months of anguish and desperation with the Mariel situation, my family called to share they had all lost their jobs. It turns out that once a Cuban resident is on the list to exit Cuba, they are all fired from their jobs. My mother, her husband, my brothers, and my sister all lost their jobs. There was a pounding desperation and our nerves started unraveling. For most of my life, I always felt in control of my emotions. But I began to feel myself cracking, wide enough to spill. Afraid I would become the mess that needs cleaning. Something happened at that moment, at that time…maybe it was a couple of things, combined together. I wasn't happy with my marriage, my kids were in their rebellious teen years, and it was a time when there was an extreme amount of tension in the household. Kelly detested (and never liked) Adrian. They were constantly at odds with each other. I believe it must have had something to do with her father, but what I'm about to share here, I know my daughter will not like this part: Adrian was not a terrible man. He helped me, and he supported me materially and economically. He was not a loving or expressive man, but he was not evil, not really. He never treated me badly, for the most part. He did have his way of being, much like we all do, but he was not a man with bad intentions. At least that is what I thought.

The Nervous Breakdown

I've never understood what actually occurred within me after the Mariel chaos, as I can only describe the events leading up to that horrible day. I've ultimately come to believe there was a hurricane forming inside my mind. Once Adrian returned to Miami, I remembered being extremely tormented by what had occurred during El Mariel. We burned through all our money trying to free our families from Cuba, leaving me penniless once more. At that time, I was paying for Lucas' medical school, as he was studying in Santo Domingo (I know, *what I was thinking*, right?). I wonder if Lucas ever understood all the sacrifices made for him to pursue his dreams of becoming a surgeon. My kids were in the midst of graduating from high school and moving towards college, and I had to face that financial responsibility alone. All I could think of was not having the means anymore to help pay for their education, which was one of my major worries; I've always wanted them to have a good education. After spending an entire life working hard and striving for the future, all of a sudden, I found myself with nothing and didn't see any way to maneuver through it. This is how depression must start.

In addition to the stress of my kids' education, paying for Lucas 'school, all of the intense days leading up to and during the Mariel, worrying about the arrival of my family, the failure of them not being able to leave Cuba, and thinking what they were going through, caused a flood of sentiments steering me to taking some medication, which I have no recollection how I obtained them, called Ambient. I think those pills must have messed with something inside me causing a negative effect on my mental state. I remember on that particular day feeling extremely depressed. I decided to go to the backyard and work on the garden. After some time of me sitting on the grass like

95

a zombie, I began fervently digging out weeds and immediately started weeping as I pulled each one, all the while repeating,

"*I'm killing the grass. They are all dead.*"

I don't recall who saw me first if it was Adrian or Kelly (although, my daughter said it was her, as I entered the kitchen through the back door from our yard), and I was hysterically crying over the dead grass in my hands. She lovingly led me to my room and laid me down. Kelly was deeply unsettled seeing me in that state, which was totally out of character for me. She went back to the kitchen to ask Adrian (who heard the commotion) to call a doctor, to take me to the hospital, but Adrian refused. He repeatedly said *to calm down, that it was nothing, and that he had it under control.* All the while, I was in bed under the influence of that medication for the immense stress I was experiencing and was never really present for what transpired in the kitchen. I remember Kelly speaking to me, something about her dad who was coming to pick her up because she was leaving. I remember being confused, asking why she was leaving, her screaming it was either *"Adrian or me".* She was frantic when her father arrived to take her away. I was imprisoned in a nightmare, unable to return to my waking life.

(Kelly's recollection of the incident)

I remember being in the kitchen making a sandwich when my mom came in through the side door of the kitchen, which led to the backyard, hysterically crying and cradling blades of grass in her hands, screaming that she killed the grass. I held her and tried to understand what was happening to her, but when I looked into her eyes, it was as if she was not there. I slowly started guiding her out of the kitchen towards her room down the hall as I called out for Adrian. He ran to the kitchen to try to determine what was happening to my mother. My mother started to melt in my arms, I was completely shaken witnessing my mother in that terrifying state of collapse that I begged Adrian to call 911— but he refused. All the while yelling at me to calm down, that nothing was happening. But something terrible was unraveling, my mother was having a psychotic episode. I turned and grabbed the kitchen phone, which was propped on the wall by the refrigerator, to call an ambulance when I felt his hand yank the phone from my hands and rip it off the wall.

"You are not calling anyone!"

With trembling urgency, I grabbed my mother's hand and ran to her bedroom and locked the door. She collapsed on the bed while I desperately tried to express how scared of him I was, but she was totally out of it, so I decided to call my brother, Carlitos, to come and help us. Adrian busted the door open to their bedroom and continued to grab me to stop me from calling anyone. Luckily, I was able to reach my brother, who was visiting his girlfriend, and desperately asked for his help. In a furry I ran out of their room and into mine, as it was next door, but he grabbed me by my hair causing me to almost lose my step. I managed to escape his grasp and ran down the hall when he tackled me mid-hallway causing me to fall backwards. Before I knew it, he was on me, pinning me down and choking me. His hands felt like cold steel. I could smell the cigarettes and liquor evaporating from the sweat of his neck while he pressed harder, tears streaming down my cheeks, I prayed he would stop. God heard my pleas and sent Carlitos, who was the first to arrive, by slamming open the front door. Once he saw Adrian in the hallway on top of me, savagely choking me, he screamed like I've never heard my brother scream,

"Get away from my sister or I will kill you!"

I felt his grip soften and I took my first deep breath of air. Once I was free from his grasp, I ran to my brother's arms. I've never felt so happy to be alive. I thought that was the end of me, but God had other plans. My brother was my hero. Carlitos, in such disarray, asked me where our mother was and I motioned into their bedroom, as I couldn't find any words to utter. My brother found my mother in a comatose state on the bed in her room. I'm not certain how my father found out, I believe my brother must have called him because he shortly arrived along with the police. I can only imagine the anger my father must have been feeling, knowing his ex-wife's husband almost killed his daughter. The control he must have demonstrated to stop him from killing this man was something to respect. As the police escorted Adrian away in handcuffs, and while he passed my way, he muttered under his breath, looking at me with evil eyes,

"If I ever see you again, I will kill you".

Those were the last words he ever said to me. That memory will never be erased from my mind and sometimes, I have nightmares about it.

I'm sorry I didn't understand what you were going through, Mom, and yes, Adrian was not a terrible man, but what he did that day scarred me for the rest of my life. I'm deeply sorry you went through that, I wish I would have understood all the pressures you were under, maybe I could have helped. Please forgive me, but I don't regret fighting for you. I would do it again and again. I love you.

The Beginning of the End

As I think now, how traumatic those days were, things still feel foggy, and I'm left still wondering. I've never truly recollected the exact memories from that horrid day. I never considered the kids leaving was going to be indefinite. Kelly leaving, especially, I thought it to be another one of her dramatics. She was an extremely hard-headed young girl with a grand imagination. I believed she would be back. Once the police took Adrian and Carlos took Kelly, I figured she would only be at her father's house overnight and return the next day. But the events that followed caught me by surprise. I was living a nightmare I couldn't wake up from.

Early the following day, I received a call from Carlos where he was hesitant to explain what had occurred the previous night in his house with Kelly. I felt a tremble in his voice as he began to share the details of her state of mind—her swallowing some pills, and falling unconscious, which led her to be admitted in the hospital, to have her stomach pumped. I was in a daze, still unable to process what was happening to my daughter. I became even more worried about her. Now, remember, I had no recollection of the events that occurred the day before. Adrian requested that we both go to the hospital and see what really happened to Kelly, and I agreed to go with him. As we entered the room, she became uncontrollably erratic and refused to have Adrian in the room. She was hysterical. I didn't realize I made matters worse by bringing Adrian. I felt trapped in confusion. On the brink of total collapse. Kelly was adamantly reluctant to return to the house. She made it clear it would either be Adrian or her when she repeated,

" I will not return as long as he is there."

I believe she feared for her life, and knowing this wrecked me.

When I got back home, my son expressed to me,

"If Kelly leaves, I will leave too."

I remember thinking to myself, *now the situation has become quite ugly.* Both my kids wanted to leave me. I called my father in Puerto Rico because, in the condition I was in financially, I was unable to do anything without his help. After hearing all the events that had unraveled, he immediately flew to Miami. I remember him picking me up in his big Cadillac car, and when I entered, his voice fell,

"Clarita, what is happening?"

I explained the situation and he said these words that echo in me still:

"Put things on a scale and the one that weighs the most, that is your answer."

I told him that I didn't need to put things on a scale, as my kids are what weigh the most. If they don't want to return as long as Adrian was there, then I would have to tell Adrian that he has to leave. I explained to him that my financial situation was very precarious and I couldn't maintain the house and the kids. He assured me not to worry about that, that he would help me. Throughout my life, my father was my lifeline — always there to save me. *God, do I miss him.*

Now came the hard part, which was to confront Adrian and tell him what was about to happen: I wanted a divorce! When I returned to the house that day, I laid it all out -

"Carlitos is leaving. Kelly is not coming back home. They gave me the option to choose between you and them, and for me, there is no doubt, I choose them. We have to end our marriage. And you have to leave."

He took it horribly, as I expected. He said my kids were unfair and ungrateful and that he did not deserve that. In some obtuse way at the time, I agreed with him, not quite truly knowing the full details of what happened the day of my breakdown between him and Kelly. That put a wedge between me and my daughter for years. Life is strange…why had I not believed her recollection of that day? Why did it take me years to write my story and have my daughter read it and discover I truly had no memory of those broken moments? I sternly repeated that he had to go, and he finally accepted

"I will leave."

The worst was over, or so I thought.

On that day, I moved all my personal belongings out of the primary bedroom and slept in Kelly's room. My nerves were on pins and needles. He wasn't very agreeable during those days. He started drinking excessively, even more than usual, becoming quite violent, of which, at this point, I was terrified. I would lock the bedroom door for fear that after he got home from heavy drinking, he would get vicious and hurt me. That's how the days followed, with tension at home escalating. I was worried my state of mind would snap again. He would assure me he was searching for a place, but it was all a lie. He would go to Olivia's and Alo's, some old friends of ours, and spend the day there. One night, Olivia called me with concern and said,

"Adrian just left our house very drunk. Please be careful and do not confront him because it will get ugly."

I hid all night. Like some sort of prey animal.

The next day, I finally gathered enough courage to approach him. I demanded his foul actions be stopped and to take control of his anger. I shared my fear and that I couldn't keep living that way. He *had* to leave. He snapped back,

101

"You know what? This is my house, and I'm not leaving. If you don't want to be with me, the one that has to leave is you."

I became very agitated, uneasy, and enraged. I'm not sure what I did or said to him, but he grabbed the telephone from the kitchen wall, took the cord, and wrapped it around my neck. The same phone he ripped off the wall days before.

I screamed…

"If you kill me, you'll go to jail."

He stopped his instinct to choke me and in that moment of facing the potential of death head-on, I've never felt so clear. I was going to make sure this would never happen to me again. I was determined to get him out of my life.

I was on the phone with my father, describing what happened, almost as if it were outside of myself,

"Dad, this man doesn't want to leave the house. In fact, he said that the one who had to leave was me, but I don't have the means or know what to do."

He told me he would pick me up the next day to search for a place. We found a cute apartment in Kendall. Unfortunately, I couldn't pay for it, but he insisted on sending me $200 a month towards rent. He stated firmly that he'd help until I could establish myself and be on my own again. Obviously, what I needed was to put the house on the market and sell it. Fortunately, the house was held jointly. The deed was in our names, which, in reality, we both worked hard to maintain. I planned, as soon as the house was sold, to have enough money to finally find some peace. I gladly rented the cute apartment in Kendall (a new two-bedroom apartment on the third floor with a small balcony). My father retained an attorney friend of his who initiated divorce proceedings immediately. When Adrian was served with divorce papers, you would think the atomic bomb went off with his reaction. He undoubtedly re-fused to pay for the divorce and insisted it would be my bur-den. He rattled on, stating that since I was the one who wanted to separate, I should cover it. I remember telling him that if he didn't want to pay for it, it didn't matter because that wasn't going to stop me from making it happen. I set off to find a way, and God provided.

While all this was happening, Kelly and Carlitos were living with Carlos. In order to see my own children, I had to visit them at their father's house. I felt like a stranger, as if I had let them down. I longed to have my children back home with me.

On the day we were set to move, I called my son to join me in renting a U-Haul. I remember Adrian screaming at the top of his lungs.

"You are not taking everything!"

He felt I should only take half of the things in the house. He demanded that half was his. In retaliation for leaving him, he kept all my children's home movies. He was vile and vindic-tive. This pained me enormously, but eventually, years later, I was able to retrieve them. Adrian couldn't disguise his ugly side and the evil man he truly was. The man he was hiding from me. The man Kelly saw. They say splitting up lets you see their true colors. His repulsive behavior was one of the toughest things to witness because I never thought he would be as vengeful as he was. He, being delusional, thought I was leaving him because he was old, and I had another man. He couldn't fathom that my kids were the actual reason why I was leaving him, he kept insisting they were just an excuse. He fired away mental abuse, emotionally sucker-punching me with each word he shouted, breaking me into pieces. All the while knowing none of it was true, but since he was hurting, he wanted to hurt me. He went as far as making a list of all the personal items I was allowed to take—a list I still have today. A list that reminds me of my resilience. He noted: there are ten plates, you take five. There are three planters, you take one, I take two. In the end, I took the dining room table, Carlitos' bed, half of the linens and towels, half of the kitchen items, and nothing else. With only those items, I vacated the home I had lived in for ten years, but in reality, that was all I wanted. With an emphasis on just getting the fuck **out** of there.

When we arrived at the house, with the U-Haul, I was quite frightened that Adrian would get physical with Carlitos, like he did with Kelly. My heart was pounding 100 miles a minute as Carlitos and I tried to take the things out of the house as quickly as possible. Thinking back, I feel quite sad that I subjected my son to that, but I didn't have anyone else that could help me. Carlitos handled it like a true gentleman, and just like that, we packed up and moved to our new life in Kendall. I never looked back. Finally, tasting the freedom I'd been searching for.

Infatuation Becomes Real

After 1980, which was actually after the Cuban Mariel, I divorced Adrian and moved with the kids to the apartment in Kendall. At the time, I was driving an old car in need of new tires. I remembered that Tomas had a tire company (we had remained in contact throughout the years), so I decided to call him. Once I told him about my car he jumped on the opportunity.

"Come and bring your car so we can get you new tires."

A couple of days later, I visited his store, and he allocated new tires to my car, refusing any payment.

"This is a gift from me because you deserve it and more. I want to take you out to dinner, have a drink, and keep in touch with you."

I didn't hesitate to accept,

"Sounds good."

Venturing into unknown territory, I thought, *tread lightly*.

We arranged to meet, all the while skirting around the fact that he was happily married. As you may recall, Tomas was an unread chapter in my young life that vanished for years, making it easy to erase his current relationship from my mind's existence. We were feeling the same emotions: two souls yearning for closure, innocent. Thus, we planned to meet one night at the exact hotel I stayed at the previous time, the Ramada, which I remembered played lovely soft music at night near the bar. There, we enjoyed dinner, some drinks, and the usual exciting conversations. Undeniably, it began, like two moths to a flame, we fluttered our dance of words, stories, and memories as if we had never parted, as if years had not stolen this moment from us.

That night, neither of us entertained the thought of a personal touch. Our minds melted together in a different form of intimacy. At the end of our evening, we planned to meet once more, respectfully. However, my body knew he craved me physically, just as much as I craved him. That next time together, we would finally succumb to our cravings, forgetting our reality for just one moment of our dream. He owned an apartment, which was vacant on 7th Avenue in the Northwest area. He instructed me to meet him at his apartment and handed me the address, sweetly mentioning it had a nice pool. I wondered if he was attempting to persuade me to join him, not realizing I would never say no. As you might imagine, I headed towards Tomas' apartment, and as I stepped in, I noticed we were finally both, alone in a room just for us. My vibrating body felt electricity as we slowly undressed, and he grabbed me into his arms, closing the gap of longing that had kept us burning for years.

Strangely enough, after we physically collided, the strong feelings of desire simply disappeared. For years, I carried this grand romantic illusion of pure adornment for Tomas, only to realize I didn't feel the same anymore. Confused as to how this could happen, I asked myself a thousand times, *why?* A man whom, through the years, I believed to have loved. Post our physical expression, I no longer had an urge, a yearning for him. Leading me to question,

"Was I a terrible person?"

Or did I create this grand romance in my mind? But then again, maybe the difference in age at that moment was much more notable. Maybe now I wasn't that innocent, dumbfounded girl who fell in a trance with an older man. I was now a mature, independent woman with a better knowledge of the world. I think in my own way, I will always have a deep sense of love for Tomas, but the thought of him leaving his wife made my stomach ill. I would never destroy a marriage. The fantasy died at that moment and the little girl in me was now a realist.

After that last encounter, he remained in touch, usually by calling about two or three times a week. I imagine he would hide from his wife to speak with me. One day, we went out to lunch, and I translated my soul,

"Tomas, this is not going to work. You are married with a lovely family and I don't feel the same as I did when I was 15 years old. I would like to keep in contact with you as a friend, as you hold a special place in my heart and are also quite important in my life, but that's all. We can't have a relationship, because it will not work."

He responded,

"I understand Clarita, the last thing I ever wanted to do was cause you harm. I always tried to protect you."

I knew that to be true because, as a young girl, he could have taken advantage, but instead, he respected me. I will always appreciate that.

Shortly after that decision, he asked to see my mother, Lola. By that time, she was living in an apartment by 7th Street (having brought her out of Cuba) it gave her immense happiness to see him. I'll forever carry in my heart that memory of my mother that day, and how she lit up reconnecting with someone from her old neighborhood in Cuba here in the States.

Hello Kendall

Me in the Kendall apartment

We moved to the Kendall apartment in January 1981 with a rent of $450 a month, which was not much, but then again, we are talking about 1981. It was a charming two-bedroom apartment with a bathroom and a small kitchen. We decorated it rather cute, purchasing a bedroom set for Kelly and I, being there were two bedrooms. The other bedroom went to Carlitos. We bought a tan sofa bed, a couple of wicker chairs for the living room, and a small round glass table for the kitchen. However, the television we owned previously was ancient. There wasn't much to move, as Adrian controlled everything I was allowed to take. In that cozy apartment, Carlitos, Kelly, and I focused on establishing our new lives. I believe we lived there for around two years. That first year was, thank God, a pleasant year, and somewhat tranquil. We enjoyed living there and loved meeting all the interesting people along the way. With my salary from The Travelers and my father's $200 barely being enough to maintain ourselves, I managed to find a part-time job at Zayre's to supplement my finances. Once I finished at Travelers at 4:30, I would head to Zayre's to work till closing and start over again the next day. Life, right?

Top Left to Right: Eli, Martica, Carlos (Pachily), Me and Taty in the Kendall apartment

Financially, it was a strenuous year, but emotionally, we were good at being together as a family—even when our kitchen suffered. Kelly would get home from school, go directly to the kitchen, open the refrigerator, and give out her staple, saying,

"There is nothing to eat in this house."

Coincidentally, my cousins (Ani, her husband Mandy and her brother Carlos, who was nicknamed Pachily) had arrived from Cuba, not long after we moved to Kendall. Ani, her husband, and my cousin arrived with his wife to stay at my apartment; countless nights, they would sleep there. We would place sheets on the floor, or they would sleep on the sofa, and there we would accommodate ourselves. Most of the time, the apartment was full of people. It was a good time, due to the family growing closer. My brother would come over with his girlfriend, Tati, who was charming and funny, my sister would come over—we filled our place with vibrant life. The fact that we had little money was evident, causing Kelly to start working and Carlitos to also find a job. They both had their part-time jobs in order to pay for their own expenses because I, honestly, could not provide everything with what I made. They learned young to work for a living to help support the family. My kids were wonderful, I felt lucky to be loved so deeply by them.

During our time in that place, several important events happened. Kelly graduated from high school and was dating her future husband. With the help of my father, we were able to buy her first car and help her begin college. Carlitos already had a car, which was bought by my dad when we lived in Westchester. Some time had passed since the El Mariel incident and since my family was still in Cuba, I became desperate, having no job and them longing to leave, specifically my sister Dulce. She would torment my mother constantly, making my mother, in turn, torment me. The calls from Cuba became constant; mind you, the calls from Cuba practically were uncommon. Therefore, my mom would call me crying and begging to take them out of Cuba. I would explain to her that it was not the best time, that I was newly divorced and had no money, but it landed on deaf ears. No one cared; they simply wanted to leave, putting me between a rock and a hard place. I saw myself being responsible for the obligation to get my family out of Cuba. The fact was that I had no means to do so. Again, I reached out to my father in Puerto Rico and shared everything that was happening, knowing he was the last person I should be asking to get my family out of Cuba. He and my mom never had an amicable relationship. I promised him that once the house sold, I would pay him back every cent he spent getting them out. He agreed and asked how much it would cost to get them out of the island. My father was always there for me and ultimately, he was the reason the Silva family all live in the United States.

Mr. Import and Export

When I lived in Chicago, I met a man, Eloy, who owned an agency that was called *"El Almacien"* which shipped packages to Cuba via Spain. In those days, there weren't any other means of sending items to Cuba directly from the United States. While supporting my family in Chicago, I was also supporting those family members who remained in Cuba. I would constantly ship them packages of clothing, medicines, and other items which were most in need. The man who owned the agency would come to my house with his son, who was a spitfire and no pleasure to be around. When my kids saw him, they would hide under the bed to avoid interacting with him. Eloy would come over with some catalogs, and I would simply pick out what I wanted to send to my family in Cuba. Cuba was in a dire state of desperation, wherein the people needed even basic items to merely survive, and I was happy and able to help them, come hell or high water.

Eloy eventually moved to Miami and opened his own agency. In addition to sending supplies, he would advertise the ability to help release families from Cuba through third-world countries, which was the only way to get out of Cuba, nothing direct. Learning this, I immediately went to speak to Eloy, as it had been years since I hadn't seen him. He was quite attentive and polite, treating me with kindness but with a splash of flirtatiousness, as he was a bit of a romantic. When he inquired about Adrian, I explained we had divorced, and I noticed his eyes bulged out while sharpening his teeth, much like a wolf staring at a hen pen. I shared with him my desperation in organizing to retrieve my family from Cuba and bring them to the United States. He agreed to help me for a nominal fee. In my mind, I already knew what his fee would be.

In the coming days, he reached out to invite me for lunch and, in the process, to share some information he gathered about the Cuban extraction process. I agreed to swing by his office, but he abruptly said,

"No, I can pick you up for lunch."

A free lunch sounded appealing, so I agreed. He was a kind man, without physical flair and well established financially. I had become tired of having a partner who struggled in that department. After that first lunch, our lunches became routine. At the start of the courtship, which was coincidentally my first date after getting divorced, was when I began to casually date for the first time in my life. The relationship with Carlos while in Cuba was constantly monitored via chaperones, never truly being alone to discuss who you were, what you liked, and if you were a good kisser. I rarely dated before he and Adrian, never having an opportunity to meet men, date, get wine, and dine. In reality, Eloy was the first. Wine and dine me, please, and thank you.

He was a generous man who would bring me gifts and show up at the office with flowers, which I would wear all day. It was quite embarrassing, if I must say, when he would gift me an orchid, I would have to pin it on like I was a quinceañera and go out to lunch with him, parading around with the orchid as though it were an ornament (and I was some sort of Christmas tree.) One day, he saw I didn't have a watch and I explained that my watch met its demise. At our next lunch meeting, he appeared with a watch to give me. *El senor me colmaba de regalos*– it got to the point where he didn't know what to give me. Meanwhile, all along, I was preparing for my family's trip out of Cuba through Panama, which was the only place to go through at the time. My mind was occupied with getting shit done, no time for *kissey, kissey*. I remember one day, while in conversation, I casually mentioned my kid's television was damaged in the move. To my surprise, shortly thereafter, Kelly called me at work, describing a man at the house delivering a television. I instructed her to tell him it was a mistake because I hadn't ordered a television. The man insisted it was for us, and it was under my name. I instructed Kelly to accept it, and we would find out what happened later. Of course, I thought to myself, who would it have come from, but Eloy? He sent us a humongous television, which I ended up owning for about 15-20 years. As a matter of fact, I decided to endure his advances, even though they weren't disheartening, and accept his gifts. It wasn't something that fascinated me, but seeing all the attention he was giving me, I accepted it. I deserved it.

Trip to Panama

In hopes of not dragging on this part of the story, I'll tell you that the moment finally arrived when my family was able to exit Cuba through Panama. Prior to receiving that news, one day, my mother called me, sounding extremely strange. I asked her if anything was wrong, only to have her shake it off. It was quite unusual for my mother to call, as Dulce was always the one who made the call, so it was natural that I would request to speak with Dulce. My mother nervously whispered that Dulce didn't want to come to the phone. *What?* I immediately demanded to be told what was going on, and she responded by saying they had a problem. It seemed my sister had changed her mind about leaving Cuba. I was shocked and insisted she explain the sudden change of heart when she was always clear about leaving. She went on to explain that Dulce had fallen in love with the bus driver who rode her to Havana when she had to go make the exit arrangements. So now she wanted to stay and marry him. *Shit!* I became enraged, as you could imagine, because she made my mother crazy wanting to leave Cuba, which in turn made me crazy as well. I stressed that we could not lose the money we paid for her ticket, it was all arranged. I asked her who else wanted to leave and take Dulce's place so that I would speak with Eloy to change the name on the ticket if it was possible. My brother Tony immediately said yes, he wanted to leave. I left to speak with Eloy about it all, to which he informed me that it would be a little difficult, but he would try to change it. Finally, he was able to do it. Because of this incident, it delayed the exit a few more months, which also delayed my relationship with Eloy. I had to wait until all the paperwork was completed, prolonging the doomed relationship all through this ordeal. I'm focused and determined at this point—*eyes on the prize.*

At last the day arrived when my family would exit Cuba. My mother and Antonio were to leave first, since the paperwork for Tony would take some time. They would arrive in Panama alone. I was worried because they were old, had never traveled on an airplane before, and were arriving to an unknown land. I had to look for a place for them to live and accommodate them there. When Eloy saw me with all the stress on my mind, he told me not to fret and that I could go and help them. *With what money?* I didn't even have enough money to buy food for my house. He offered to buy the ticket to Panama for me. I refused, but he insisted, and honestly, I did need it, so I gave in and accepted.

When I landed at the airport in Panama, I hailed a taxi to head towards the address I planned to stay at, which turned out to be an apartment building that had some rooms to rent, being that I could not afford a hotel. When I handed the taxi driver the address, he was skeptical…

"Ok? Perfecto."

When we arrived, as I was exiting the cab, he asked me if I was going to work there. I was confused,

"No, I'm here because my parents are arriving tomorrow from Cuba and I'm picking them up."

I asked him why he thought that, and he replied,

"Because in this building, many women of the night live and work here."

It, allegedly, was seen as a building full of women of the night (prostitutes) who would rent out the rooms, hence why the rooms were so cheap. He made it known to me that when Cubans arrive in Panama, they stay here, having no knowledge of this place. Regardless of the warning from the taxi driver (I was too exhausted to care), I stayed the night and, the next day, went to the airport to pick up my mother and Antonio. We all stayed together there for three or four days while I got them settled. I was able to connect them with other Cuban families, including a family from Pinar del Rio that they knew. I left them there and returned to the United States. My stress level was reduced by maybe 10%.

Mom's Arrival to the United States

My mother, Lola, and her husband, Antonio, lived in Panama for around two months. During those two months, I helped them financially with everything. Sending them the little money I had in order for them to get by. Who would have prepared me for their arrival in Miami and the stay at my house to be exhausting. To begin with, my mother was never an easy woman, but I hoped the years changed her, like they change all of us. After all, I was not the same. Well, I was still a bit argumentative, but not as much as I was when I was younger. In addition to that, my mother arrived very disheartened, as she practically came under obligation because her beautiful daughter, Dulce, who wanted to leave, didn't end up leaving. The time she lived with me in Miami —God forgive me —was a torment. Lola made everyone's life extremely difficult. She would spend her days crying in a corner, lamenting and complaining. She wanted to return to Cuba and didn't like living in an apartment. She was accustomed to a different way of living, and I understood that, but I also understood that I was her daughter and that she had grandkids here, and that I had made an enormous sacrifice, one which she had no idea about, in order to get her out of Cuba. I was devastated seeing my mother suffer and hoped she would recognize how much I loved her. I empathized with her pain of missing her home country, it hangs heavy like a neon "vacancy" sign on your heart. But I also know the power of moving forward.

I found Antonio a job as soon as I could with his friends at La Casa de Capo. I also trained him on driving and the rules of the road (who would have thought I would be teaching someone else to drive.) I would drive him to work in the beginning until he got the hang of it, as he did originally know how-to drive-in Cuba. The owner of La Casa de Capo was a close friend who gave him a car, which was a relief for me, resigning as chauffeur. Angels walk among us, people, have faith. He finally sprouted into independence. Once he started working, his oldest son, Tony, arrived in Panama, and he took it upon himself to care for him. They couldn't repay me financially because, with the little money he made, he used to help Tony and maintain themselves with daily needs.

The situation with my mother became unmanageable, and although it pained me, I was forced to ultimately request they move out. As a matter of fact, one day, she said she wanted to go back to Cuba - I lost it and responded by yelling,

"When? So, I can buy your ticket and you can go."

Antonio begged me to have patience with her, but I remember explaining to him that she had made my home a place of suffering. Everything was negative and my kids shouldn't have to be going through this. Shortly after that conversation, they found a place to live, and they moved out, which, in the long run, was the best plan for all included. After they left, my cousin, Pachily, Ani's brother, had gotten divorced from his wife and was living with some friends, uncomfortably, so I offered for him to come to live with us for a while until he found a place to live. Shortly after my parents moved, Pachily moved in and the kids loved him.

Pachily was a young, creative Cuban actor/artist with a cultured, worldly essence about him (his father was a famous Cuban actor) who arrived at my apartment to stay for a bit, but in reality, he stayed until we moved out of the apartment. My home was like honey to people, and we were the revolving door. I failed to mention that by the time my mother arrived and everything was established, I ended my relationship with Eloy. I didn't share his same sentiment and refreshing enough, he understood. My person was out there, I was positive about that.

The Wild One

A few months later, while I was working at Travelers, there was a co-worker named Jony. His personality was infectious. He was versatile with the guitar, loved to sing, and raced cars in Daytona. I was enthralled with his bad side. He stood a medium size, 5'9" with brown shaggy hair and mysterious brown eyes. We would have lunch together while at work, and eventually, we began dating. He was a bit of a rebel, rode a motorcycle and completely enchanting. I could spend hours listening to Jony recounting his adventures. He was from a wonderful wealthy family with immense status, but he was, missing a screw, something I learned was dire, as we grew closer. He became dependent on our friendship, being that we were more friends than lovers. We never shared bodies together, meaning we never had sex, if I must be blunt. Although there was a date wherein he attempted to kiss me, since I knew he was in love with another woman, I refused his sexual advancement. From that moment on, we were simply good friends. My connection to him, other than enjoying his company, was joining him on his spontaneous adventures of living life on the edge—something I only used to do out of necessity or survival, now I did out of leisure.

One day, he asked if I wanted to ride his motorcycle, and without hesitation, I mustered the courage to wear a helmet and ride his motorcycle. I was hooked. We would go everywhere on it, so much that I didn't recognize myself. As we rode the motorcycle through Key Biscayne and other places, he would fly through the streets while I was secretly freaking out, clutching to him for dear life, scared to death, but loving every second of being alive. If Johnny needed me because he was depressed or was going through something, he would call me and I would drop what I was doing and lend an ear. That was the kind of relationship we maintained.

It didn't last long, for many reasons, but mainly because he was not in love with me, and I was not in love with him, nor did I want to be. We both knew this. I admired him as a man and as an exciting person. He fascinated me with his wild personality, but I knew there would never be a happily ever after love story for us. Ours was merely an adventurous relationship. Knowing our time together was finite, I eventually ended our friendship. He accepted it quite well, to my surprise. Many years later, I learned he was in jail and had lost his mental capacity for life. It was a terrible misfortune to discover what became of him and his story. I find myself, from time to time, honoring the gift he gave me, which was the desire to live my life so unquenchably full.

The Party Man

Months later, my friends Lilly, a big, boisterous Cuban woman with huge breasts, and Herman Solo, a loud fast-talking Cuban man with jet-black dyed hair, introduced me to a friend called Javier. They met Javier in one of their gatherings and spoke to him about me, sharing that I was single and a friend of the family, and asked if he could take me out dancing. They wanted to play matchmaker and shortly introduced me to Javier—a tall slightly slim man with dark hair and gold brim glasses. We shortly began attending parties together. He was a dancer and loved to dance in different styles. I, on the other hand, did not hold that same love for dancing, so right off the bat, we lacked chemistry. He was young and a bit hyper and loved to party. Although with him I did attend the only two concerts I'd ever gone to in my life, Julio Iglesia and El Puma. He was basically a partner solely for outings. If I were invited to a party, I would take him, and if I didn't dance, he would dance with anyone there. If he had a party, he would take me and show me off. He liked people to see him with me, I was his party doll. Being from a different world, all this was new to me, and I pushed myself out of my shell a little bit more to grasp at life's little treasures.

One day, Javier hosted a party at his residence, and a friend of his started chatting with me. The gentleman asked where I worked and I mentioned I worked at The Travelers Insurance Co. As soon as I said it, he blurted out that he knew a friend who worked there called Mayra Perez, whose husband played baseball with him. He requested that the next time I saw her, to share that a man called "*El Buey*" said hello. El Buey was with an American blonde voluptuous woman at the party, and I was with Javier. Similar to Jony's relationship, I never had sexual relations with Javier. I wasn't interested in that kind of relationship with him. I admired the fact that he was always happy, well-dressed, and on the move, never having met someone like that in my life. That's the side of him I liked: what I've never had. As my luck would have it, he also was not looking for a sexual relationship. I never wholeheartedly knew why. Maybe he just wasn't that into women? Or me? Regardless it wasn't really a puzzle I felt down to solve.

Since there was a lack of chemistry or even a *spark* of chemistry with Javier, our relationship failed to blossom. Although I did enjoy our time together, having experienced the party life, which I was not accustomed to, sadly, after that night, I ended the relationship we shared and simply continued as friends. This relationship made me realize life can be for pleasure, not just work.

I share the memories of all these men merely to show a glimpse of how they have all played an important part in my journey. People come in and out of your lives for different reasons. You take what serves you and filter out the rest.

Teenagers Are Fun

Martica and Carlitos in Kendall

During the time we lived in the Kendall apartment, Kelly had her first official boyfriend, Alec—a short, cocky, fancy-dressed young man who loved the nightlife. They didn't last long, being that he cheated on her. He was caught walking hand in hand with a full-figured, dark-skinned girl through the Calle Ocho parade by Kelly's uncle, Gallego, whom she loved dearly, who later called Kelly to share the new insight about Alec. Months later, she fell in love as all teenage girls do with a boy named Ray, a sweet boy with long curly hair, who played drums in my son's band, which included Charly who was Carlitos best friend. Charly was a quiet boy with shaggy messy hair, hippie attire, and round 'John Lennon' spectacles that fell midway down his nose as he spoke. That relationship with Ray ended before it began, since he left her for his former girlfriend, whom he previously dated for over five years. He broke-up with Kelly over the telephone. I remember feeling her anguish for weeks. She mourned that breakup for a bit and slowly moved on by falling in love with Charly, who, as we recall, was also a member of the same band (and Ray's best friend as well.) Teen girls are complicated. Carlitos was passionately devoted to music, having taught himself how to play the guitar at a young age. He was heavily involved in the music scene with his band. When we lived in Westchester, Carlitos found his first girlfriend, Martica, a beautiful, smart, stylish girl with sassy, short black boy-cut hair, who went to school with Kelly (they were close friends) and was in her modern dance class. Carlitos met her one day when Kelly gathered a group of her dance class girlfriends to the house for a meeting. Kelly recalled to me how at that gathering, Carlitos asked Martica what her favorite song was, and she said shyly, 'Stairway to Heaven which he immediately began playing on his guitar, starting a relationship that would last his entire life. Kelly became Charly's girlfriend and their story continued through the years, and each flourished separately at the end.

Kelly and I in our Kendall apartment on her graduation day from high school

During the time we lived in Kendall, Kelly pulled on all my emotional strings, handing me obstacles and countless headaches with her teenage antics. I remember her being involved with a group of girls that, in my opinion, were all wild and crazy. Against my better judgment, she decided to stay friends with them. When Kelly's party days initiated and she started venturing out late with her wild friends, before the time of cell phones, there was no way of knowing where she was or when she would return home. Sometimes, arriving hours past her curfew, and sometimes, she would not come home at all, which caused countless nights of torment thinking of all the terrible things that could be happening to her out in the streets alone. Like everything in life, it passed and our life continued. She grew out of the phase and into another. Thank God Carlitos didn't go through those phases. I could only handle one wild child at a time. We argued a great deal, but we also were thick as thieves.

"El Buey" The Beginning

Oscar and Me

We were smack in the middle of 1982 by now. One day, while in the lunchroom of The Travelers, with my coworker friends, which included Mayra (the head of the personnel department) who, as you recall, hired me, she would occasionally join us for lunch. However, on that day, she sat at the table and instantly inquired,

"Are you dating anyone?"

I had just recently ended that strange relationship with Jony, which, by the way, none of my friends or family members had approved of and would constantly criticize me about dating him.

I countered,

"No."

To which she pursued,

"Are you no longer dating that crazy fellow, Jony?"

I confirmed it ended, and I definitely was not seeing anyone. With keen interest, I questioned why she was asking. She described that the other day, a friend of hers came to her place and was curiously asking about me. I repeated with some doubt,

"A friend of yours asked for me. Who?"

She responded,

"Do you remember that guy that you met at Javier's party who they called El Buey?"

I took a moment to recollect,

"Yes,"

She shared how he visited her and wondered about me. I probed with confusion,

"Why?"

She went on to tell me that he remembered me and thought I was charming. She suddenly had a quick thought—

"I can host a party at my place and invite him over again."

It was around the time of my birthday in August. She volunteered to have a party at her place and invited a few married friends, and included him. She planned for me to go and get to know him. I politely said,

"I'm not interested. Nor do I want to meet anyone new. I'm good at being by myself."

She insisted;

"Don't be dumb, come to the house and allow yourself a good time."

I ultimately caved, although still unsure if I should go.

The night of the party, I had no yearning to dress up, as I was merely going to a friend's house, where all the guests were married. Even though that man was going to show up, I actually had no recollection of how he looked like, nor any desire to impress him, so I didn't put much of an effort on my appearance. I made my entrance when Mayra was preparing the food. There were two other couples, Gloria and Pablo, and Ani and Leo, when I arrived. Sometime later, almost at the end of her setting up the food, the famous El Buey arrived. He entered like a tornado through the door, carrying a bouquet of flowers in one hand and a box of cigarettes in the other. He greeted us by giving me the flowers and Mayra the cigarettes. Needless to say, I was impressed with his entrance. I did not anticipate that. His stature was six feet, athletic type, dark brown curly hair with small sideburns, and a smile that melted your heart.

El Buey was quite entertaining. He was much like me, vivacious at heart. Although he did remind me of a Cuban comedian named Alvarez Guedes, who wasn't so charming. He made us all laugh during the night, extending practically till dawn. We all sat on the floor recounting stories, listening to music, and drinking champagne. At one point, the men went to El Mutiny (a famous club in Miami) to hunt for a couple of bottles of Dom Perignon (apparently one of the highest champagnes), which for me was new and unexpected. I felt right in place, or maybe it was the bubbles tickling me from the champagne, but whatever it was, it was magical. We cheered, we drank, and everything was perfect. When dawn was nearing, everyone started retiring. I lived far from Mayra, she lived in the Northwest, and I in the Southwest. Being we were all drinking through the night and it was still a bit dark, El Buey glanced at me and spoke,

"By the way, the famous 'El Buey' is "Oscar."

He continued to say,

"If you prefer we can leave to my house, which is close. That way you can stay until the sun comes out and then go home."

Although Mayra assured me it was safe to leave with him, as she vouched for him, I had my doubts for a man who was a stranger to me. She added that he had a big house in Coral Gables, lived alone, and was a decent man. Nothing would happen unless I wanted it to happen. I thought that option was better than driving my car at that late hour and under the influence all the way home, so I went with him. Coral Gables was in an exceptionally high-class area, *it should be fine*, I kept telling myself.

His house was straight out of a fairy tale. It didn't impress me too much, but it did leave me wanting something like it one day. The front welcomed you in with tall green trees and groomed busting bushes in a row towards the doorway. The oak wood door hardly ever opened, guests would always enter through the side kitchen door by the alleyway. We entered by the side rear of the house, which was inconveniently dark, and through a room that displayed two tires from a deserted car, I would assume, thrown in the middle of the empty room. I pictured myself in a maze trying to escape unhurt. He cradled my hand as he led me to another room. This time, it was a bedroom—his bedroom. There was a queen-sized mattress on the floor, and the room was adorned by a small television propped on an empty milk box. It was quite depressing, actually. This is where my mind began to raise some concerns. He assured me not to focus on the state of his house, as he had recently moved in. Ok, this I understood. He went on to explain that the house was his and his wife's, who had recently moved out, and he stayed with the basics, having her take everything. I was somewhat relieved. He didn't want me to spiral and decided to put my mind at ease by offering that he would sleep on the sofa in the living room, while I slept in his room. I was exhausted from the night of drinking, so I agreed. I threw myself on that mattress on the floor, fully clothed with shoes on, only to be awakened minutes later by a cockroach crawling all over me. It completely freaked me out, grossed me out, and sobered me up. I quietly tip-toed to the living room, tapped him on the shoulder while he was dead asleep on the couch, thanked him, and left. Who needs to wait until sunrise when you've got cockroaches in the house?

The First Date

As you can already ascertain, my first encounter with Oscar was less than glamorous, and certainly no fireworks to talk about, well maybe with his cockroach. The following day, I had an engagement with Mac, a Jewish attorney with a full head of dark straight hair, square glasses, and a slim build who worked at The Travelers. Mac previously invited me to attend an event at the Jockey Club, a place I'd yet to visit. I was delighted to go and was excited to celebrate my birthday. It was going to be our first outing together, although we had spoken several times via phone and had seen him a couple of times, I couldn't pass up the opportunity to enjoy The Jockey Club. Our date was set for the next day, wherein he would pick me up at my house. Coincidentally, that day, Oscar called me stating I had forgotten my sunglasses at his place. He mentioned he needed to pick up his son and could swing by to drop them off. I agreed to let him drop them off, since I did need my sunglasses. My thought was he would swing by, drop them off, and leave on his merry way. To my surprise, when he arrived later that afternoon, he casually sat making himself feel at home. Kelly had the television on; seeing her, he asked to change the channel and put on a baseball game instead, which they both started watching. I interrupted him and explained, excusing myself, that I was waiting for my date, who was on the way to pick me up, and I needed to finish getting ready. Nonchalantly, he dismissed the interruption and assured me it was fine for me to continue getting ready as he happily sat watching the game, all the while having conversations with Kelly and Carlitos, who had joined in.

I left him on the couch, went to my room, showered, dressed, and dolled up for my date. All this time, I thought he would leave at any moment, but to my surprise, he didn't. So much so that he was there when Mac, the attorney, my date, came in, and I found myself introducing Mac to my kids and Oscar, who shook his hand in acknowledgment, all the while on the sofa chatting with Kelly and Carlitos. Once the introductions were over, and thinking Oscar would leave at that point, not seeing him move, I motioned I was leaving and Oscar nonchalantly said goodbye and that he would leave as soon as the baseball game was over. With that, I left with Mac to The Jockey Club, which turned out to be a disaster. I must say, I thought about Oscar all night.

Mac was extremely unpleasant and unlikeable. After I had my first drink, he never offered me another one. We ate and drank what we had, not sure if we listened to music. He gave me a tour around the club and took me home. When I arrived at home, obviously, Mac was history. There was nothing I could learn from him except that he was boring, and that I didn't want to be.

When I arrived at the office on Monday, I immediately saw Mayra, who, as you would guess, asked me what I thought about El Buey. I shared with her I honestly wasn't quite impressed with him (yet secretly I was). Oscar was good-looking and had a magnetic personality with tons of charisma. Mayra emphasized that he was impressed, even asking her to invite me over to her house again (we were like two young, giggling girls learning that a boy has a crush on you). She mentioned they were getting together again this weekend. They all loved baseball and there was a game they wanted to watch. She invited me to join them. I hesitated and explained again that I wasn't impressed with Oscar "*El Buey*", but since I had no plans, I ended up attending Mayra's party that weekend to see the game.

Let me summarize briefly: the house I listed for sale in Westchester (which was the house wherein my kids, ex-husband, and I lived) we assumed it would sell quickly. It was, however, actually the only house in history in the area that took forever to sell. I thought I was cursed. That house was listed for two years before it finally sold. Adrian would always enact roadblocks to prevent the house from selling. He went as far as bringing his ex-wife, a terrible, mean, vindictive woman, and daughter to live in the house. I was later made aware that Adrian gave my clothing, which was still in our closet, to his daughter, because his ex-wife was large and the clothing didn't fit her. He planted roots in the house all the while avoiding to sell. Finally, after multiple back-and-forth arguments with Adrian on selling the house, it sold. Coincidently, it was around the same time I met Oscar.

At that time, my means of transportation was falling apart. I was deathly embarrassed to drive the 1974 Buick with cracked leather, no heater or air conditioner, and worn-out paint, held together by duct tape for fear someone would see me. I desperately needed a new car. When the house was sold, the money I received from the sale was divided into three parts: Kelly, Carlitos, and me. The money I gifted to Kelly and Carlitos was in hopes they would save it for the purchase of their first home. They were preparing for their weddings and the joy of helping them start their new lives together brought me warmth. The money I kept was to purchase a new car, which, between us, I secretly always wanted a new car. The best thing I did was share my good fortune with my kids.

I'm not certain if it was that following Sunday when I went to see the game at Mayra's house, but throughout this time, Oscar and I had been chatting via telephone. One day, he invited me to lunch; I remember being oddly nervous, like a schoolgirl with her first crush at lunch. Needless to say, Oscar and I were on our way to getting to know each other. While at

Mayra's house watching the game with Oscar and the other guests, I was hoping I could go afterward to visit a car dealership, but since the dealers always took advantage of women and since I wasn't educated on buying a car, I asked Oscar who was sitting next to me and intently staring at the game, if he could accompany me to the dealer to buy a car. He agreed to take me after the baseball game was over. His team won. We headed to the Toyota dealership and he helped me purchase a new car. I love being taken care of, but also being my own woman.

Our courting after that became a little more formal...wink...wink. We entertained copious amounts of sex. On Sundays, he would invite me to the park where his team had a baseball game. I gradually started meeting all his friends at these games, and as time would show, I began to like him more and more. I learned that everyone who knew him knew he was simple, down-to-earth, honest, and charming. On one of our dates, he left his Ray-Ban sunglasses in my car. The following day, I was invited to a pool party at my friend's house, Olivia and Aurelio, which coincidentally was also on Sunday. I explained to Oscar that I would not be attending his game that Sunday, as I had a pool party with friends to attend. He was strangely calm and wasn't upset about it. I found this a bit peculiar because he loved having me at his games. I brushed it off (like most women do). When Sunday came and I entered my car I noticed his sunglasses in the front dash. I decided, since the park was on my way to the pool party, to swing by and drop off his sunglasses to him since he would be there.

When I arrived at the park, I noticed the atmosphere was tense with all our friends. I could feel their eyes on me. Otto, his son, avoided me when I arrived. At that moment, I sensed something was awry. Instead of leaving, I wanted to stick around a bit to discern what was causing the uneasiness. I sat on the bleachers next to a couple who were his friends that I had previously met. I remembered the woman was from Puerto Rico who sat next to me and heard me say I had to leave for another event, when she abruptly turned around, insisting I not leave. I explained I had a previous engagement to attend, nevertheless, she insisted I stay. At that moment, I noticed Oscar sitting at the dugout and thought this was my time to go and give him his sunglasses. As I approached the dugout, I noticed him a bit fidgety. As I reached to give him his sunglasses, he turned and nervously said,

"I thought you weren't coming today."

I responded nonchalantly,

"Neither did I, but I saw you had left your sunglasses in my car, and I thought to bring them to you before my pool party, but I think I'll stay now and watch the game."

I noticed him flinch again.

What I wasn't made aware of that day was that Oscar had been secretly dating a tall, blonde, curvaceous American woman who lived in West Palm Beach, while he had been working there. This American woman coincidentally was called *"Clara"* just like me. What are the chances that a man you are dating is also dating a woman with your same name? Who does that? It turns out Clara was visiting him at the game that day, sitting on the bleachers. After I finished speaking with Oscar and returned to sit next to the Puerto Rican woman, she confessed to me, while pointing,

"That woman over there is Oscar's girlfriend."

Nonchalantly again, I responded:

"Oh, really, then I'm going to stay right here and see what he does after he finishes his game."

I was on a mission, and no one was going to tear me away from that game.

Once the game finished, apparently Clara noticed something weird was going on (women have amazing intuition), as I had done, and since everyone was being quite obvious about the situation at hand, she went down to the dugout when he came out, they spoke for a second and then she left. Usually, after every game, the team sets up a dominoes table under a tree and spends the rest of the day playing dominoes. I loved that they repeated this tradition. It was a weekly tradition, which he deeply enjoyed. When I saw them sat down, I approached Oscar.

"Hey, I'm leaving."

He sarcastically remarked,

"Now is when you decide to leave?"

I blurted out,

"Yes, I have a party to go to."

He fired back,

"Now you should stay the other woman left."

Don't tempt an angry woman -

"What do you mean the other woman left?"

My Latin blood was boiling. Oscar immediately went on to explain that he and Clara were going out, but it was over. She only came to the game because she had an idea that Oscar had left her for another woman. When she saw me, she knew. He asked that I stay, and since I felt victorious, I stayed. I won the game that day, but somehow my heart felt sad for that beautiful blonde woman. Who am I kidding? Gane!

Coral Gables

The Bulls Inn Gang—Left to Right: Ramon, Jorge, Albertini, Oscar, El Magnifico and I

After that incident, things progressed quite quickly; dating turned into sleeping over at his place, seeing each other more often, and treating me as his partner. It was perfect learning how at ease I felt around him, smooth and comfortable with him, as if life was lighter, easier. Oscar was not typically a man who showed affection physically, he was instead noble with his affections displayed through small-unnoticed gestures. He wasn't detail-oriented, but he was wonderful, mischievous, and fun. I did envision he could be my future.

Our courtship continued, and at the end of the year, around December, the landlord notified me of his intent to raise my rent in January. I was, unfortunately, still with few financial abilities after having paid my father back the money he lent me to get my mother out of Cuba. He did leave me off the hook for the money he was giving me monthly to help pay for my rent, as it was a gift for me. In reality, I had paid all my debts, but I was still living paycheck to paycheck. The financial struggle was taking its toll.

When I shared the news with Oscar that my landlord was going to raise my rent, he offered for me to move in with him. He went on to say that since he had two empty rooms, each of my kids could have their own room, and all I had to pay him was $200 a month towards rent. I requested that he give me time to speak with the kids to see how they felt. Kelly had already planned her wedding for the following year, and Carlitos was planning a wedding for the near future as well. Since both of the kids were eventually leaving, I would have stayed alone in that apartment, paying a high rent, and with an empty room. The math worked. When I spoke with Carlitos and Kelly about moving in with Oscar, they were both excited. They liked Oscar from the first day they met, especially Kelly. She saw a father figure in him, one who gave her his time and listened to her struggles, and never judged her. They both agreed and loved the idea of having their own rooms and living in a house in Coral Gables. Soon after, we moved the bit of furniture we owned into Oscar's house and started our lives together. I was happy. We were happy. Life began making sense again. We were all working towards our future together.

Oscar was an avid sports fanatic. He loved sports from an early age and enjoyed a game of baseball every week with his friends, sometimes two to three times. He played basketball, racket ball, hell, every different ball game. He watched and attended baseball, football, and basketball games basically any sports event. Once I met Oscar, my life drastically changed, from lacking any knowledge of sports to being the center of attraction in all pre-games. I explored learning something new and, in the process, fell in love with sports. The majority of Oscar's friends were males. Some of them were married by the time we were together, but for the most part, the majority were all single. My friends were an eclectic group of fun, intelligent, married, and single women who loved music, dancing, drinking, and traveling. As my world merged more into Oscar's, we created our own adventures together. Over time, some of my female friendships naturally faded as my interest with them did. Soon, Oscar and I were enmeshed, and I could've lived that way with him forever.

Being both Cubans and lovers of games, we began hosting a Dominoes game night at the house on Sundays. I suggested the team come to our house after their baseball game, as there was air conditioning and they would be comfortable, instead of at the park, sweating buckets. This dawned a new tradition. They began coming to the house on a regular basis. At one point, they recommended changing game night to Friday nights, which slowly became a routine. I remember having the best times during those Dominoes games. We drank, we smoked, we joked, we danced, solidifying our special friendships. We were a big group that lasted for several long and happy years. I loved the idea of having Oscar home instead of out and about. Through the years, I became a master at playing Dominoes. The guys at first weren't happy with my participating, but they had no choice in the matter; after all, it was our house, and I ruled, or should I say *we*. The Dominoes club , which we christened the *"Bulls Inn"* was official. The Bulls Inn got enormous momentum, sometimes having around 14 to 16 men attending the game night well into the early morning on several occasions. Everyone maintained different occupations and lives, but when they all united for a game of Dominoes, it was as if they were all one grand group of best friends, friends who ultimately grew old together and watched each other succumb to death. I miss them all—Their infectious laughter and lingering scent of cigars.

Did I mention how Oscar got his nickname "*El Buey*"? It was while he was playing baseball in Mexico with his team and not because of his floundering ways, but because it was a Mexican term for "*dude*" or "*bro,*" and it stuck.

The Trip That Almost Ended Us

We were perfectly happy in our relationship until the beginning of 1986, when things went awry. One of Oscar's friend, not one that participated in Dominoes game night, but one he knew for several years proposed to Oscar a trip via train for some illegal dealings, not sure to where. The memory of that particular scenario is hazy, but I did remember that Oscar had mentioned to me in passing the offer they made, which he was considering. I was completely against the idea from the beginning. I stressed to him that he absolutely didn't have a need for it, nor take any chance to ruin his life, since he had a good job. I also had landed a good job with high pay, positioning us in a comfortable financial position. In addition, the risk was too great, possibly going to jail and losing everything we worked for. I stressed the immense disagreement of the whole matter.

Oscar, first of all, was a person who was not entirely expressive; he wasn't a communicative person, and secondly, he was a bit sneaky (the one quality I didn't admire about him— everyone has one of those). He eventually decided not to go on the trip. But a few days later, I asked him what finally occurred with the trip and his friend. He responded vaguely as if he wasn't sure he was going to go through with it or not. I couldn't believe he was still thinking about it. I declared these precise words to him

"Oscar, if you go forward with that plan, I will leave you. I refuse to live with the terror of thinking I have a man next to me that can possibly go to prison, nor can live with a man that ends up in jail. If you decide to do it, I will leave."

Talk about being dramatic *(I picked it up from Kelly)*.

The following weekend, Oscar brought his son Otto home, as he often would, picking him up Saturday morning, driving him to baseball, and returning home, where Otto would stay until Sunday night. That weekend proceeded nicely, we went to bed on Saturday night happily, but when I woke up on Sunday morning, Oscar was gone. There was only a note next to me instructing me to please drive Otto home, as he had gone to the place where he needed to go. He would call me when he arrived at his destination. You can probably imagine my reaction at that moment. He was stealthy, quietly packing at night and leaving. I became incredibly enraged with him, but more so by the fact that he didn't have the courage the previous day to inform me of his final decision. His action hurt me deeply, causing me to rethink my entire situation with him.

The next day, as promised, Oscar telephoned to share that he had arrived at his arrival point. I asserted,

"Our relationship is over. When you return, I won't be here. I never want to see you again. We are done!" (dramatic, but justified, I thought)

He was speechless and probably didn't quite believe me. Needless to say, that was exactly what I did. I'm a woman of my word, once I say something, I do it. I shared with the kids what had occurred between Oscar and I (not sure if I told them the truth or made something else up-don't judge- we've all been there), explaining to Carlitos that I was leaving and I wanted them to leave with me. Pushing my grief aside and being the Virgo that I am, I immediately found and rented an apartment nearby Ponce de Leon and 8th street all while he was away. Women can accomplish anything, especially when there is a heartbreak and a goal.

I was again in a pickle, because we had planned to have Kelly's wedding reception at Oscar's house to save money, but due to me having to rent a one-bedroom apartment, we needed to find another place. Unfortunately, we didn't have any spare cash to rent a reception hall. In addition, since I was only paying Oscar $200 a month for rent, and the apartment I finally rented was for $600 a month, I was again struggling to make ends meet. Carlitos was also in the process of planning to get married the following year. Therefore, I had the notion that once Kelly got married, Carlitos could come and live with me.

There I went again, creating chaos for my children by asking Carlitos if he could stay with his father for a few months, just until after Kelly's wedding, when he could move in with me in the one-bedroom apartment. This decision devastated me, breaking up my kids over an argument with a man. I found out years later when Carlitos confessed to me one day of being angry with me for throwing him out and for never calling or checking in on him while he was living with his dad. I was horrified to learn this, especially since I never expressed to him what I was going through at that time. Kelly's wedding was rapidly approaching, and I had no idea what to do about the reception since I was in the process of mourning the breakup with Oscar. And let's not forget the lack of financial instability I was facing alone. At the end of it all, Carlitos had no other option but to live with his father. I pushed to create a normal, stress-free life. Sadly, and regrettably, Carlitos never returned to ever live with me again, causing a severe strain in our relationship for years. Looking back at how I behaved in those moments leading up to my children's division, I can only ask God for forgiveness and pray they also forgive me for my actions. Flawed as I am.

The Impromptu Separation and Quick Return

I wholeheartedly didn't know what my kids thought of that most unpleasant situation, although I truly wished I did. We never spoke about the details or had a deep conversation together. I believe we all lack communication skills, especially with matters of the heart. I realized in our family, we were never encouraged to express our true emotions or have soulful exchanges about our mindset. This was something I wished had been done in our household. Buried inside, I felt as if Carlitos resented me for asking him to move in with his father. I don't think he ever knew (and I never shared with him) that it took everything I had to ask him to go. My reasoning, silly as it was looking back, was that since Carlitos was 22 years old, had a job, a car, and was already, what I deemed, a man, he could survive it. Never did I think about his emotional state or what that would do to him. I only thought of myself and my outrage with Oscar. I would, without a doubt, have preferred him to stay with me until he got married, but that was not in the cards. I will say this: Cuban parents love for their kids to live with them until they're old or no longer need to live with them. My heart splintered and contorted with the regret of that decision my entire life.

I swiftly left for a friend's house, Carlitos went to his father's house, and I don't recall where Kelly ended up, but I knew she was safe. All that to say, Oscar returned to an empty house. I wondered what he felt the moment he walked in and found me and the kids gone. Oh, to be a fly on his wall. I took that opportunity to rent a U-Haul. There I was again, with my poor son helping me get all the furniture out of an ex-lover's house. I needed to break this pattern. I needed to depend on myself. I needed to shelter my kids.

In the days when Oscar returned, after I no longer lived there, an unusual event happened. I was informed, although I deeply wished it wasn't true, that Oscar had moved a random woman into our house, or should I say his house. I could only imagine, in my wild and mad imagination, that she must have been a prostitute, not that I have anything towards that profession or an escort of high quality, but in this case, Oscar and his friends were messing around with a wild woman. On the day I arrived to get my things out of his house, I couldn't take much as my apartment was tiny, just Kelly's bed, having to leave behind my living room and bedroom set. I also wanted to take the recliner I had gifted Oscar on our first Valentine's Day. It was a double. I really wanted to take it with me, but I only wanted one side, and in my fury, I was looking for a way to split it up, but it was futile. In the end, I took the entire recliner. I also took the sofa cushions and left the sofa, out of spite, as I was furious. I did manage to squeeze in the small dining table, which really didn't fit in the apartment, but over my dead body I would leave it behind for them to use for their enjoyment. I was clouded with pain so there was little air for clear thoughts. *Hell hath no fury like a woman scorned.*

Carlitos reluctantly, which I understood, joined me in moving out the furniture, but surprisingly, when I returned to the house and entered the bedroom, I found that scarlet woman sleeping on what used to be our bed on my newly purchased sheets, which I had just picked up for added flare to his masculine room. I was furious (my Cuban temper came out to play) causing me to, in a state of wrath, grab her by her arm, pulling her out of what looked like a drug-induced state. With the strength of Zeus, I managed to drag her out to the living room, threw her on the sofa, and went to the kitchen to grab a knife. Carlitos saw me grab the knife and must have thought I was headed towards the woman, but instead, I was actually heading towards the bedroom to cut into shreds all the sheets that she was lying on. I'm not a murderer-or am I?—No, no, of-course I'm not. Being in a state of immense emotion, all I was thinking of was those sheets that I bought and where Oscar and I had our last night together. I remember ripping the sheets to threads with the knife like a maniac-*who was I?* Once I totally destroyed the sheets, I pulled off the curtain from the living room windows that I had sewn, all the while still under a spell of pure anger, and demolished them. Carlitos, at this point, was in a state of shock seeing me irate and softly asked me to calm down, emphasizing how unhinged my behavior was, as he nervously instructed me to

"Get what you need and let's go."

We loaded what was left on the U-Haul and left the disaster I created behind. All the while I was in my manic state, that strange woman just lay on the sofa. I wonder now what she must have been thinking. Maybe she was thinking-*don't mess with a Cuban woman.*

When I was driving on Ponce de Leon towards my apart-ment, I noticed Oscar pass me in his van, which was easy to recognize, and as we passed each other on the street, the only thing I could do was stick my head out of my car and scream.

"Motherfucker!"

I didn't regret doing it because I was totally destroyed, but today I would have handled it differently. It's true time matures us. I ultimately forgave him and moved back, but the damage to the kids was already done. As parents we try our best to shield our kids from hurt, but as an individual, we try to shield ourselves.

The most frightening and embarrassing thing for me from that unflattering encounter was that my kids witnessed the storm within me, seeing how out of control I was while feeling

146

used and destroyed. I was in love with Oscar and couldn't understand the way he acted with no remorse as to how he was treating me. It crushed my soul. In some way, through this book, I hope to ask for my kids 'forgiveness for having to make them weather such dark seasons in their lives. But, as we are all human, with sentiments that cause us not to be rational, I only hoped they would ultimately understand. I don't regret leaving the house, I only regret how I behaved. During those three months I lived in that lonely apartment, I cried every day, suffering greatly, as I still loved Oscar. It took a long time for me to understand his actions. I always assumed he was under the influence of drugs and his friends, but I truly don't know. It's still quite difficult to share what he did and what I did.

After three long months, he called me one day. I don't remember for what, with some lame excuse *(as all men ultimately do...right?),* which eludes my memory at this time. On other days, he would leave me messages, as well as his friends, pleading for me to return. He would say,

"No one is living at the house anymore, and everything is back to normal. Please think about it. That's your house too."

I was not ready to return to him, but Kelly's wedding was quickly approaching and I had zero cents saved to be able to pay for Kelly's reception, nor had any ideas of where to have her reception. I did know I wanted to gift her at least a small gathering, even if it was with just family, which is how it ultimately ended. That fact is one of the reasons why I was motivated to return to Oscar's house. It was one of those things that I knew I needed, and since Oscar was already asking me back, I felt I had to do it for Kelly. Sometimes, we have difficult decisions to make in life, and understanding the reasons why makes it easier.

One Friday night, he appeared looking for me at my apartment saying,

"Let's play Dominoes together. Our friends miss you and they want you to join us again."

I responded by asking,

"You?"

He coolly replied,

"Me too. Now come play Dominoes."

He picked me up and drove us to his house, where all his friends were. They all greeted me with much love. Everybody, according to them, missed me. They knew I was good for Oscar. They knew he needed me to keep him healthy and out of trouble. *He needed me.*

That night, I played Dominoes with them, and when the hour came that everyone left, I urged him to take me home. He asked,

"Why don't you stay?"

I quickly said,

"No! I'm not that easy. Take me back home and I will think about whether I want to return at all. I'm still extremely hurt."

He begged, he cried, he showed his vulnerability, stating he needed me.

"Please forgive what I did to you. Please come back to live with me."

I still left, sharing with him that I would think about it. When I arrived at the apartment, Kelly was there, and I shared everything that happened that night, hoping to get her opinion. Kelly, from the start, deeply loved Oscar. I think it was the fact that he treated her like his own daughter. She said,

"Mami, go back to him. I'm moving out after the wedding, and Carlitos doesn't want to return to live with you."

So, eventually, I found myself back with Oscar. This decision was the best decision I'd ever made for my kids, their kids, and ultimately me.

Oscar and Me

Kelly's Wedding

Left to Right: Me, Kelly, Charly and Carlos at the
Coral Gables Congregational Church

Once I envisioned having a girl, if only to splendor her with a lavish wedding, like in the fairy tales I read about. Alas, this was reality and not a fairy tale. As I mentioned previously, instead of gifting her the money for her wedding, I gifted it for the down payment on her first home. Much like most women raising kids on their own, I had little help, including from her father, who at that time was unable to help me financially with Kelly or Carlitos. He was in the middle of his own family drama. When we divorced, he was ordered to provide me $40 a month for both kids. Now, thinking back, I believe that amount was minimal. That was in fact, what the Cuban divorce court ordered. In Cuba, $40 was enough, but here in the United States, to maintain and raise two kids on a measly $40 a month was laughable. At that time, he was living in his house on Kendall, and Carlitos had already turned 18, but Kelly still had a couple of years to go. That was the moment I decided to take Carlos to court to increase the kids' alimony. He did give me more, but I don't remember how much. It was only for a short time, and only for Kelly, since I waited for years to take him to court, he didn't have to pay for Carlitos, as he was 18 already and of legal age. It worked out, Carlos was always around if I ever needed anything for the kids.

Nonetheless, Kelly's wedding turned out lovely. We settled on having the reception at Oscar's house with all our family. Barbara, Charly's sister-in-law, who was a smart, sensible, and kind woman, lent Kelly her wedding dress, which had a lovely vintage style with lace and flower embroidery. Although Kelly preferred a new dress, she looked angelic and eventually secretly loved the dress. Her hair was styled like a movie star to one side, her makeup was radiant, and the veil was attached to pearls which wrapped around her head, creating a godly essence, much like that of the Lady Madonna. I, being the mother of the bride, would have loved a new dress as well and been able to go to a beauty salon, but again, my financial situation wouldn't permit it. I ultimately wore a purple satin dress with shoulder pads that I stored in my closet for years, which was not the best choice, especially after seeing all the wedding pictures. I looked like a pregnant Barney doll. I styled my hair by teasing it high on top and straight on the bottom, and applied my own makeup. I still felt like a queen giving away her princess. It was a magical moment.

The day of the wedding was spent running around searching for flowers, finding a cake, scrambling to gather everything, all the while decorating the house. This left me little time for myself. Even though it was Kelly's day, I secretly longed to look perfect for her. In the end, everyone had a marvelous time, and more importantly, Kelly was happy. My little girl did get her fairytale wedding—just on a budget.

After Kelly's wedding, life returned to normal with Oscar and I beginning our lives together again. I was employed at an insurance company managing the personal injury claims department of 18 employees earning a moderately high salary, (I believe to have reached the pinnacle of my career, starting at the bottom and little by little working my way to the top) and Oscar driving for a large apparel company with his own route. Life was good, and the kids were content. This is how the American dream felt like.

Me at Latin American Ins. Co.

Happy Days/ Not So Happy Days

Me holding Huston

On September 1, 1985, Kelly married, and on January 2nd, 1989, she had her first baby boy. I shall never forget that moment in time, while Oscar and I were at a party at Zule and Robert's house (Zule was my best friend and her husband Robert), I received a desperate call from Charlie informing me he was rushing Kelly to the hospital because she was in labor. Her water had broken, and he was frantic, mainly because she was a month early. Oscar and I immediately headed towards the hospital, hoping we would make it in time for the birth. Kelly was a true warrior, handling the contractions like a champ, and after 13 hours of labor, projectile vomiting, and no painkillers (she vowed to have her baby all natural), she delivered Huston DeAngelo Lorenzo, a healthy baby boy, at 1:13 pm the next day. That moment in time instantly changed our lives forever. He was like the messiah being delivered at the manger with the three kings awaiting his arrival - Oscar, Clara, and Charly. He saved our lives and gave us a purpose in life. He was our little miracle baby, as my daughter had been informed early on she was unable to bear children. Huston being born was magic.

We spent the first and second day practically out of our home dealing with Kelly's new motherhood. We returned home late on January 2nd, from being all day at the hospital finally returning at night. We arrived exhausted, having celebrated New Year's Day completely without sleep awaiting for the birth. The day after New Year's, we remained all day entirely in the hospital, so when we arrived home, we were comatose. There was a rare cold breeze that night, and we thought it would be pleasant to leave the window open to enjoy the night's breeze. We opened the window in the dining room, left it open, and went to bed. We were accustomed to always, before I moved to that house, closing the bedroom door with a lock. It became a routine to lock our bedroom door, especially when the kids lived with us, we didn't want them to walk in on us unexpectedly.

The next morning, when Oscar woke, the first thing he did was head towards the spare bedroom to check our answering machine for any messages since we'd been at the hospital for two days. When he entered the room, he immediately noticed the room was completely ransacked and instantly gave out a scream, calling out for me,

"CLARY"

I leaped out of bed upon hearing Oscar's sound, dreading the worst had happened to the new baby, my heart stopped. I ran towards the room where he was in and when I entered, I instantly noticed the disarray. My heart dropped, my hands began shaking, and I was in utter disbelief at what had occurred.

WE WERE BURGLARIZED!

The criminals ruthlessly opened all the drawers of the dresser and tore out the closet doors where Oscar hid a wooden oak box with small letters in-scripted *"Oscar"* would store all his valuable baseball cards. That box was thrown on the floor, and all the cards painfully scattered all over the floor (to our luck, they were oblivious of their value). In Kelly's old room, which I transformed into a small boutique furnished with a desk to display, all the fine jewelry I was selling was gone. We reluctantly and somewhat fearfully continued throughout the house to the living room. On the table in the dining room where Oscar routinely laid his watch, ring, and wallet when we would arrive home had been left untouched. We found that strange. We continued towards the game room to find the only thing missing was a game of "*Cubilete*". Cubilete is a popular dice game played in Cuba, it's known to be played as much as Dominoes. That was the extent of their haul. I was flabbergasted.

The shock and fear we sensed, knowing someone entered our home and robbed us all the while we slept, was overwhelming. Apparently, the criminals, since they noticed there was an alarm and tried to open the bedroom door but noticed it was locked, realized there were people at home and left running out of the side kitchen door, which they left unlocked. Life saver! The moral of the story is to lock your doors!

In the scope of things, the burglars didn't take much of value, only the jewelry. This was the second time we were burglarized in that beautiful Coral Gables house. The first time it happened was coincidentally around Christmas as well. That time, they were able to take everything, including expensive jewelry from Kelly and me. Kelly was devastated to learn they had taken her gold, "Kelly" inscribed ring, necklace, and bracelet, which I had gifted her. That time, they really did a grand number on us. This second time wasn't a great loss materially, but it was still a huge impact, knowing we were at home sleeping when they were in the house robbing us. I thought of taking self-defense classes but never did.

After that day, we took precautions by activating the alarm every day, and never again did we leave a window open.

Destiny Calling

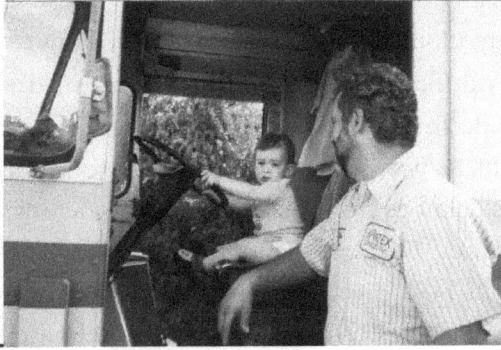

Oscar and Huston in his Aramark truck

When the moment Kelly's maternity leave was about to expire and she needed to return to work, I don't clearly remember exactly if it was weeks before or if the three months maternity leave was completely over. Still, I did know Huston was a beautiful little baby, and she didn't have anyone to take care of him while she was at work. At that moment, I made a choice—I decided to leave my job to stay home and care for Huston. This was a decision that I never regretted, and I always thank God for that blessing. On the contrary, if I had to do it ten times, I would have because to be able to give that precious little miracle the attention that I gave him. The love and care, was invaluable. I summoned the courage to resign. I was fortunate to have a good relationship with the president of the company. To my surprise, he shared with me that the company was in a bad financial situation, as it was about to go bankrupt. I went to speak with the president and told him I needed to resign to care for my grandson and that I would prefer for him to fire me instead of me quitting. This way, I would be able to collect unemployment until I was able to stabilize myself. To which he agreed. I was grateful my entire life for Mr. Ramirez.

Huston's birth unraveled a sudden 180-degree turn in my life. I suddenly found myself at 42, leaving my career to stay home and care for my first grandson. The change was difficult at first, but ultimately, after getting the groove, it became slightly less difficult. All my life, I've maintained a source of income, aside from the fact that I was currently claiming unemployment, so it was a no-brainer when I took on the opportunity to sell clothes from the house. I consider myself a powerhouse—when I set my sights on something, for the most part, I get it. *For the most part.* I persuaded myself to do it. I would buy clothing from a downtown warehouse, as I mentioned in the prior chapter, I had a boutique in the house where Kelly's room was. I would visit the insurance companies that I was familiar with and display the clothing to them to make a sale. This allowed me the flexibility to earn an extra income, all the while not feeling like I wasn't working or producing for my family. Why do we torture ourselves by thinking we can't just take a break from working all the time? Although caring for Huston was a full-time job, I would periodically take off with him in his little blue carry-on and lug him with me everywhere. From the time Huston was born, he was always my little partner. The most incredible experiences were lived with Huston while growing up, allowing me to enjoy him tremendously. I adore him extremely and was blessed to be able to have created a strong bond while he grew. I wasn't the only one who fell in love with Huston, Oscar became obsessed with him. He loved coming home from work to play with him (and sometimes, while at lunch, he would bring the truck for Huston to sit in it). The twinkle of a newborn introduced a new kind of happiness.

When Huston was about one year old, my unemployment ended. One day, while selling clothing to the employees of the insurance company, which I often visited, Ocean Casualty, the manager offered me a job to work remotely. They inquired if I could process the claims and payments of personal injury cases from home, which I instantly accepted. The process started wherein I would pick up the files, take them home, and work at night after Kelly would pick up Huston, which normally would be by 5:00 pm, but she was always late. She was a paralegal in a prestigious law firm who demanded an excessive number of hours at work. I accepted the work for Ocean Casualty, and it was good for a few months until a friend of mine called and informed me that there was a position in the office of a surgeon who was looking for someone to prepare the billing and collections. They allowed me the courtesy to choose my own hours, so naturally, I went to the interview and chose my hours, which had to be from 6:00 pm to 9:00 pm. Three jobs were better than one. The hustle is real, guys.

It came the moment when Kelly, for whatever reason, couldn't get home to pick up Huston before my work shift, wherein I would drop off Huston at Cuca's house, Charly's grandmother, who always had a concrete judgment with a dash of a silly outlook on life, and would continue to the office, which coincidentally was on the way to where I lived. I would leave Huston with Cuca, and when Kelly got off work, she would pick him up there. This process repeated itself for a few years, and both families relished the time with Huston.

On June 6, 1986, Carlitos, married his high school sweetheart, Martica, after seven years of courtship. The wedding took place at Signature Gardens, a beautiful venue which was quite popular at that time. It was truly a spectacular wedding, as Martica was meticulous with each detail. They both looked radiant and very much in love, but that is an understatement, because after 30-some years and four children, they are still very much in love.

Martica and Carlitos on their wedding day at Signature Gardens

In April 1990, my son gave me my first granddaughter, Michelle. She is the sweetest, smartest, and most dedicated person you can imagine. She became an OB/GYN and married her sweetheart in a beautiful, lavish wedding. Seeing her now as an adult, with a husband, home, and happily married while practicing medicine warms my heart.

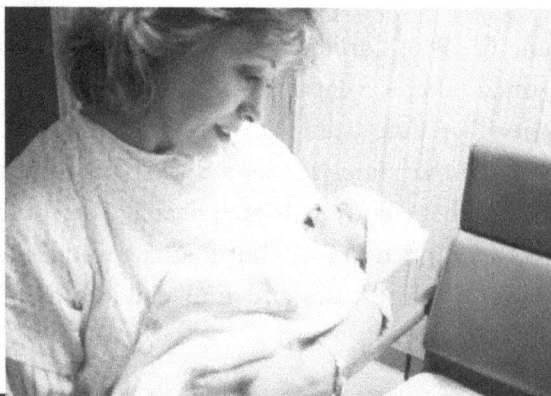

Me holding my granddaughter Michelle

Huston and Dalton

On June 6, 1991, Huston was two years old when darling, sweet Dalton was born, making him my third grandchild and the cutest, most joyous boy shining the biggest smile I've ever seen. Dalton was born on time, and again, Kelly delivered all natural and without the aid of pain killers/medications—a warrior again. Her doctor originally informed her years ago she would not be able to bear kids, he said it again and again, but God had another plan. I was devoted to caring for both boys. Dalton was lovable, caring, and loved to eat. Huston loved his younger brother from the moment he met him, and they were inseparable. I cared for Dalton and Huston when they were both babies while still working at the doctor's office. During this period of time, life became a bit more difficult trying to earn extra money wherever I could find it. It pained me to leave little Dalton and Huston with Cuca more often than not, although she loved it. Eventually there came a time when I couldn't watch them anymore, and Kelly was forced to find another alternative. My mother, Lola, and sister Dulce began caring for the boys on days I was unable and they brought a new kind of joy to their life—being able to make my mother smile. My job was requesting more hours from me and luring me with increased pay, unintentionally forcing me to accept and extend my hours, to start a couple of hours earlier. Sadly, money has a way of changing your priorities. Oscar was devastated not to have the boys around as often, but he made sure to visit them at Kelly's house every day. I felt a great sadness, as I loved spending time with Huston and Dalton. They were smart, joyful, and always loving and loyal little boys. I needed to focus on my future...for them.

Then, a year later, Kelly was pregnant again, and this time, on August 27, 1992, three days after the destructive Hurricane Andrew devastated Florida, she gave birth to Nikki, at the hospital which was running on generator power. I still remember the doctor calling her insisting she come to the hospital before the hurricane hit, as she was due any day, but since there wasn't enough room in the hospital to house Dalton and Huston, only herself, she decided to stay home with her kids to give birth in the closet if need be. Fortunately, Nikki came three days after the devastation into a chaotic world. This tiny ball of joy entered the world singing instead of crying. Oscar was over the moon the moment he held her in his arms. That little jewel was born with a brilliant sparkle shining through her tiny hazel eyes and adorned with curly chestnut hair (by the time she was born, my daughter and her husband were having marital problems. It was truly another miracle Nikki was born. All you could think of was thank God she was healthy. Thank God all three of them were healthy. Kelly had been diagnosed with an abnormal inverted uterus and was told she would never be able to bear children.

Nikki

To everyone's surprise, including her doctor, she birthed three children. Kelly has always been a strong girl. She vowed to her grandmother, Lucia, that if she ever had children, she would deliver them naturally and without any painkillers. Kelly was true to her word three times over. Spending all those years with the grandkids made Oscar and myself happy and fulfilled.

On July 1993, my son had his second child, Brandon, a shy, bright-eyed boy with a mischievous smile who would brighten any room. Later growing up to manage his own business.

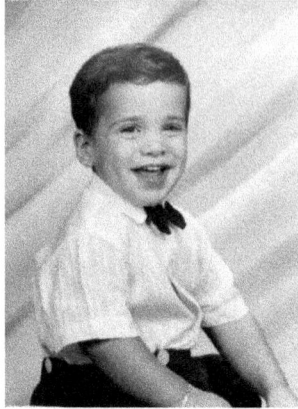

Brandon

On November 11, 2002, my sixth grandchild from my son's side, was born—Melissa, a precious little girl with curly hair and big brown eyes, born with a love for life. Another welcomed surprise came on April Fool's Day of 2004, when my son became a father for the fourth and final time (talk about an April Fool's Day surprise), gifting me with my seventh grandchild, Bryan—who was, from birth, funny, entertaining and charming. He is the life of any gathering. I'm overjoyed and proud of all my grandkids!

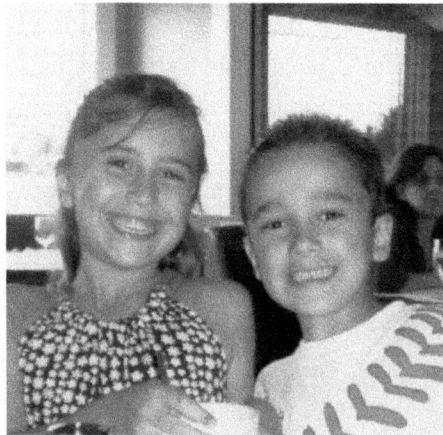

Melissa and Bryan

Infatuation's Final Farewell

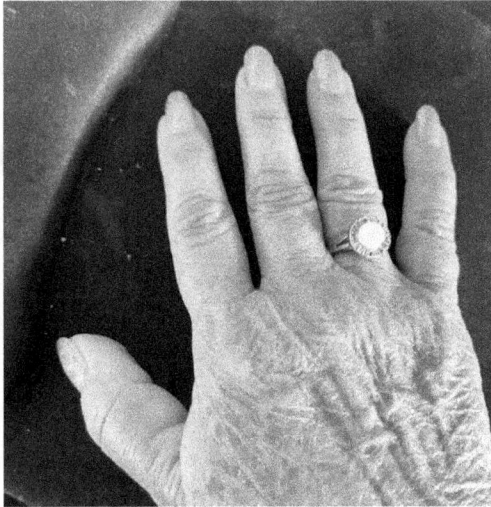

The Pearl Ring

Father Time took its toll preparing his plan. Through the years, I met Oscar, moved in with him, and was working at a quaint doctor's office when one day, Tomas and I accidentally bumped into each other coincidentally at the bank. He, without hesitation, blurted:

"Clara, I would like to take you out to lunch. Please come to lunch with me?"

I told him I was in a serious, loving relationship, and our encounter would be as old friends reuniting. We exchanged numbers again, made plans that he would call to schedule the meeting. We met several days later for lunch. This time, I wasn't nervous. I felt it was time to close his chapter.

Upon seeing Tomas again after several years, I came to the conclusion that my feelings for him would never alter. He'll always be that creative, admirable, and educated older man I once cared for. He looked older and worn out, yet still harnessing that light in his eyes. While at the table, to my surprise, he pulled out a small gold box from his pocket and said,

"Look, I owed you this many years ago."

When I opened the gold box, there inside laid a ring with a small pearl, which I still own today. My hands trembled as my eyes streamed tears of joy, leaving me quite emotional and nostalgic, staring at my pearl ring. The ring that embodied our bond in Cuba. We hugged as if we were holding on for dear life, and at that moment, we both felt how much we truly loved each other.

Some time passed after that last encounter, as we didn't see each other for some years, until one day, I would say about 15 years later, while I was working with my daughter at her title company, which we opened together and called *"Clear Title of South Florida"*.

While I was getting out of my car in the parking garage, I coincidentally stumbled onto Tomas and his wife again. What a small world indeed. I mean, out of all places in the world, he would walk into the parking garage where I worked. He looked like a small elder man by now, a man beaten down by life and age. Every time we would run into each other, we were filled with delight, as always, to see each other. Our connection was unbound electricity for eternity. As he hugged and kissed me, I felt him frail in my arms, not like our last encounter where his hug left me breathless. Excited, he greeted me,

"What a surprise seeing you here!"

I eagerly and proudly responded,

"My daughter and I own a title company here."

He looked at me for a moment before saying anything then confessed,

"I'm here because one of my doctors has an office here. He is treating me because,

(as he said these next words, my mind went blank) …

I have cancer."

It gutted me to hear him say those words, looking happy but depleted at the same time, next to his beautiful, faithful wife. It took all I had not to show how devastated I was. My knees suddenly buckled as I desperately regained my composure. I wished him the best, sent my love, and gave him the business card of our company, letting him know that if he ever needed anything, we (I) were there for him (them). I was left with immense sadness for him and for his loving wife and kids. No one deserves cancer. I despise it!

Shortly after our last run-in, he called and informed me he needed my daughter to prepare some important documents for him. My daughter was shining in her career, helping many different people with their estate and corporate matters. He scheduled a meeting at the office for him and his wife to meet Kelly, who, by the way, was eager to meet him since she knew our story and wanted to put a face to the man who stole her mother's first kiss. The joy in his face upon meeting Kelly and thinking she could have been ours together, there was still a glimmer of love in his eyes. Kelly graciously prepared the documents he needed. We all said goodbye, and he was gone once more. Not long after that meeting, I would say about a year later, he called to bid his final goodbye, unbeknownst to me. That call was our last forever goodbye, although I didn't know it at the time, but he must have. After all, by now, he was extremely ill and evidently knew he was close to death. My first friend, my first secret, my first ring was leaving this world. That day when we last spoke, I remember him laying bare his love for me,

"I want you to know that I loved you very much since the moment I laid eyes on you. Unfortunately, our destiny wasn't favorable to us due to the difference in age, but I loved you, always did, and always will. Please don't ever forget me."

Breathless, shaking with tears streaming down my face, trying for him not to hear the fear in my voice, I softly whispered one last time,

"I love you, Tomas, and will till the day I die."

Career Life for The Win

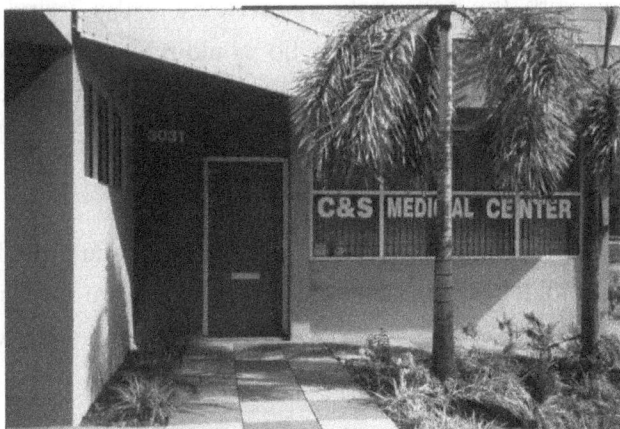

C&S Medical Center office

After six years and countless days of pondering, it occurred to me that I should create my own medical billing consulting service and get my groove back. I ventured to visit different offices of the doctors and clinics that were lawfully struggling to evaluate the functional ability of the office, give a recommendation, and charge for my services of consulting. I named that company with my father's help. He always had the ability to find the perfect names for the business (I wish he were able to help me pick a name for this book). By this time, he was beginning to show signs of Alzheimer's, of which we had no clue this was happening. When I decided to open the company, I called him and shared with him the idea. He thought it was great and between us, we decided on a name. It was one he came up with—CADUCEUS CONSULTING SERVICES. By the way, a quick fun fact: did you know Caduceus is the name for the symbol of medicine? My father was a genius and I miss him everyday, he was the smartest man I ever knew. Living those final years with him, witnessing the erosion that deadly disease brings, was the sort of heartbreak that loiters in you. It's still difficult to think or write about.

I'd like to lighten the mood at this time and talk about my professional life after I left The Travelers. When I started working with the consultation services, I had a friend who worked at an attorney's office who would refer patients to the doctor. She mentioned, in passing one day, that there was a clinic in Hialeah practicing quite badly. She thought to ask me

"Why don't you go and give them a free consultation?"

She added that they needed my services. At the time, I was driving an old, beat-up, junky car. I would perform my visits in that car—UGH. One day, while at lunch with her, she saw my car and bellowed:

"Clara, if you want to represent yourself as a woman in a good position as if to demonstrate that your business is prospering, you can't show up to places with that junk of a car. I would recommend you buy a new car."

I've always been quite scared of incurring needless debt and have tried by all means not to owe things above my pay, but she did make sense. How was I going to represent myself as an executive for my company with a broken-down vehicle? I planned on getting a new car, as soon as I could. I was determined.

I remember clearly one day, I attended my first interview with the owner of a clinic in Hialeah, and when we finished and started walking together toward my car, he gasped,

"Is that your car?"

I quickly responded,

"No, that is my daughter's car that I sometimes use it because she works downtown, and I don't like her to go with this car in case it leaves her stranded."

I was mortified and said to myself,

"I have to buy a new car."

Unfortunately, at the time, I didn't have enough money to put down a deposit. Who would you think I went to…but my dear ol' dad? I went to speak to my dad and explained the situation again, as I've done throughout my life. He, who was still doing well, said,

"There is no problem, Clara. Whenever you want to come and get me, we'll go to a dealer to pick out a car. I will take care of the deposit and will pay the monthly payments; and when you can, you pay me back."

In reality, I never did. By the time I was able to pay him back, he had lost touch with reality and did not recognize any of us. Except his wife, who, by all means, we felt, dealt with his illness and at his end claimed all of the estate. Not that it bothered me, after all, she did care for him in his last years when his family couldn't do it on a daily basis, she did it daily. When we would visit him, at times he would remember, and other times we were strangers. His health declined little by little, and then one day, minute by minute, until he was gone. I feel him in me still, all these years later. He was the smartest man I ever knew. I think I've mentioned that in prior chapters, but in reality, he was. It is one of life's many ironics that a man with such astute mental capacity would succumb to a disease that preys on that very thing.

How I noticed something was not right: On the day, while at the dealership with my Dad, I started noticing odd things he was doing; things totally out of character. For example, he would ask me several times,

"What time is it?"

I would then question him,

"Papi que pasa? Why do you need to know the time so often?"

171

He responded offensively by stating he was hungry. I assured him that as soon as we were done, which would be in a bit, we would go grab lunch. He then began to ask me where Elvira was, when would he see Elvira? I found that strange, especially since he was married to her, but I didn't pay any mind to it. Finally, we finished buying my new car, a Toyota Corolla, a Beige, four-door, fully decked out, clean car with a lovely scent, and we went to lunch to have a wonderful time together. After lunch, I dropped him off at his house. Another action he did that seemed off was when we were leaving his house and stopped at the corner, I asked him,

"Papi, is it a right or left to go to the dealer?"

and he said,

"No se."

That was a path he often traveled and knew like the back of his hand. Papi was an expert driver with pristine direction. It threw me off, not paying mind to it other than he was tired and old. Later, when he was diagnosed with Alzheimer's, I remembered those small details and wished there was a cure. I also wished I had known more about that unforgiving disease to have been able to catch the signs earlier.

I prepared a solid evaluation for the clinic in Hialeah. That office was an absolute disaster. All the files were left unbilled, it was horrible. I presented the evaluation to Art, which he read it immediately, and after reviewing it, he said,

"I would like for you to be in charge of my office, make all the decisions—you hire, fire, you do what you have to do, but I need this office to start making money. What you noted in your evaluation was very interesting to me, but I need someone to enforce it. Why don't you come to work for me?"

I emphasized the desire to stay independent. I opened my company because I didn't want to have a fixed schedule. He responded,

"Here you can have whatever schedule you want, come at the time that you want, leave at the time that you want, as long as you bring me the money that is owed to me."

He offered me an extremely high salary, including a percentage of the money I collected. It went swimmingly, and I thought the offer was fantastic. I was going to make tons of money while having the liberty of managing my own schedule. I was positive I could recover all the money that was there to process for collection, especially having the load of contacts with insurance companies I had acquired. I also had a system of collecting the money quickly. I accepted Art's offer and started working at that clinic in Hialeah.

If I remember, I started working for the Hialeah clinic at the start of the year.

Me puse mis patines—("I put on my skates" as they say in Spanish).

Right away I went into action by taking all the files that hadn't been billed and began billing them, which led to the collection of most of the money that was due. To wrap it up, by December, Pedro had already collected an impressive amount of outstanding money, and it was all because of my skills and hard work. I liked working, it gave me a sense of recognition and community. This good fortune led to him hosting a Christmas party for the staff. Pedro had me fire the woman who was his manager. Turns out, she was also his girlfriend. Now that I was having a positive impact on his company and taking on the role of manager, he had no more use for the other woman, nor was he into her romantically anymore. So not only did I have to fire her for him, I had to dump her for him too. Men, right?

I felt bad for her and wondered if that could've been me in another life. I was never one for office romances, though so…probably not.

At the Christmas dinner, Pedro stood up to say some words-

"This event was possible because of the hard work Clary had done, in which she was successfully collecting all the money that was unbilled and uncollected."

He thanked me in front of all our peers and colleagues and expressed his appreciation for my dedication to work. Between us, I was quite proud that I, a small-town girl from a distant country, was able to improve someone's business. That moment inspired me to always achieve and succeed in everything I ventured into life. Knowing I could accomplish anything I put my mind to felt empowering.

I was working with Pedro for about two years and by the end of the second year, I was running the entire business with him, not even having to visit the clinic anymore. He became quite settled and contemptuous in the process of me steering new patients, managing the office, communicating with the doctors, and preparing the billing and collection of money. In other words, I did absolutely everything, while he reaped all the benefits. Remember that friend of mine who encouraged me to start my own consulting services company? Well, one day, she did it again. She nudged,

"By the way, I think you are wasting your time at that clinic. You practically run it as if you were the owner of the business, but you're not. The one who is making all the money is him, all the while you are doing all the work. Why don't you become independent?"

I reminded her that I didn't have the money to establish a business. She told me that there was a doctor who had an office in Coral Way and was only using it two or three times a week.

"Why don't you talk to him and make an arrangement to maybe use part of the office. You can bring your own clients."

I thought about it for a minute then she continued,

"I need a doctor in the Southwest area."

Since I was in Hialeah, she had someone to send her clients there, but she needed someone in the Southwest area. Again, she had gifted me with another great idea. I extremely appreciated her for the challenge she gave me both times.

I began to consider the idea, as it seemed reasonable to me. I said to myself,

"Why not? I can do it!"

I investigated and went to see the doctor on Coral Way. I interviewed him, and he proposed to rent me the office three times a week. *Perfect.* I decided to give Pedro my letter of resignation and inform him of my plan, since honesty is the best policy.

" I'm going to open a business in the Southwest area. I will give you a month to find someone to occupy my position. I don't want you to think this is a betrayal. I know your clients are from Hialeah but mine are going to be from the Southwest area. I am not interested in taking away your business, but I do want to open my own."

His response was,

"Don't worry about anything. I'm not going to go forward with my office. When you leave, close it, liquidate everything and whatever you need from here, you can take. You can take equipment, or whatever you will need to start your business. This business does not interest me if you are not behind it."

My mind was blown, being honest does pay.

After resigning and liquidating everything from the office, I found out that the doctor was in the hospital, having suffered a heart attack. My feelings were riding a rollercoaster that had halted at the top, and all I could do was pray for some good news or to get off this bad ride.

I thought to myself *now what am I to do?* I was lost. I decided to share my predicament with Oscar who responded cool as ever,

"Don't worry. You'll find something else. Wait to see what happens to the doctor. Maybe you might be able to stay with his office."

Oscar was right—the doctor recovered from his heart attack. God was protecting us both.

When he returned to his office, I was eagerly awaiting him to plan our next move.

"What will be your position now, and what are you going to do with the business?"

He calmly replied,

"I'll leave this office because I have another office in Kendall, which is the one I will work at. If you want, transfer the lease of the office to your name, pay the rent and I'll leave everything how it is."

His intention was to leave me the office completely furnished. He added,

"Create an inventory, tell me exactly how much you think all this is worth, and you can pay me monthly for it."

That was another *"break"* life gave me. This was a man I had just met, and to my luck, he was no longer interested in the office and didn't want to stay there. I wonder if his near-death experience gave him the change of heart. No pun intended. The office was on a cute corner, fully furnished and perfect. The only thing I needed was to retain a doctor who would oversee my patients and to find a technician to administer the therapy, because everything was stocked and ready. I also needed to attract clients. Come on, let's go, Clary...*punte los patines!*

I immediately went to work by calling all my contacts, informing them I was opening an office on Coral Way and 30th. They all agreed to work with me, as I had an honorable reputation in the insurance profession with the doctors, attorneys, and professionals. I challenged myself to be respectable to everyone, and in return, they all responded positively. When I spoke with the doctor who worked the Hialeah clinic, who by the way, was an older doctor who worked certain days out of the week, one day at one clinic and one day at another, I proposed to him an idea

"Dr. I am opening this office and I was hoping you can come one or two times a week to see my patients. Give me a break and see how much you can charge me for this. Please help me."

I felt confident in asking, having worked together two years in the Hialeah clinic. He said,

"No worries, I will start going once a week and according to how your clients go, I'll go more times a week."

To not prolong this story, the birth of C&S Medical Center commenced. Later, I created a diagnostic company, which I called *"CCS Diagnostic Center."* My journey working at the Coral Way clinic was on its way. I started acquiring new clients, and thanks to God, all went relatively well. This adventure went on for about two years.

Did I mention that in the process of running the clinic, I performed every single management, medical, and office duty needed to operate the business while taking care of my grandchildren? At the start of the clinic, the state required all clinics to have a therapist on-site. Coincidentally, I was informed by the schools specializing in massage therapy that before they graduated, they are required to perform voluntary hours in a doctor's office. Therefore, I requested that the campus send me students to perform their therapy sessions at the clinic. It was a perfect set-up; they would show up and perform the therapies, and I didn't have to pay them since it was all voluntary work for school credits. I gradually learned how to do the therapies myself. As I mentioned earlier, I prepared the medical reports, worked the billing, scheduled appointments, cleaned the office, and catered the coffee. Basically, I did everything again, but for myself. I was working without employees for some time, until the business started picking up, wherein I hired a woman to do the therapy, but I kept doing everything else. When I didn't have patients, I would still stay at the office until late and come in on the weekends. A good worker produces good results, and I intended to get the whole kit and caboodle. I was the captain now!

The clinic produced quite well for a couple of years. Until the time came when, after some unexpected changes in my personal life, I decided to sell it. I spoke with the doctor and detailed the reasons why I was selling the clinic, and if he knew anyone who was interested, to keep me posted. He responded,

"I might know someone in one of the places I work who may be interested. I will talk to him."

Eventually, again, everything came out perfectly well, thanks the heavens. The man came, he liked the clinic, and I left him with everything, as was done to me previously. Pay that shit forward!

Once the doctor was paid, I liquidated all his stuff. I left the man everything, even the active patients. He paid me and assured me he would have the rest later once he received some finances to come through. In the end, I never recovered the rest of the money he owed me. I have a strong belief God returns everything good, and by some means, the money was returned, but not by pursuing that man to pay me what was due, which was not a lot.

All in all, I laid C&S Medical Group to rest and bid its final farewell in this Chapter —grateful for its metaphorical bones that held me together in its stride. I learned a great deal about myself as a woman (and business woman) during that ride.

The Nightmare Begins

This chapter is, quite frankly, the saddest chapter of my life. In the year 1997, Oscar was diagnosed with carpal tunnel syndrome from his hands falling asleep, which made them extremely uncomfortable. We saw a hand specialist who informed him he needed surgery on both hands. We went to the hospital on the day of the surgery, and during the pre-op examination, the doctor explained his failure to perform the operation due to his blood pressure, which was overly high, accompanied by a small fever. He recommended Oscar to see a cardiologist in order for the cardiologist to give him the authorization to move forward with surgery. Once he would get the clearance, they would operate, but in the meantime, the doctor would not subject Oscar through surgery under his condition. We made an appointment with a cardiologist because, throughout all this time, Oscar had never needed a cardiologist, even though he had suffered from high blood pressure since he was 18 years old, attributable to kidney problems and years of body abuse. Evidently, he had a minor renal deficiency that caused his high blood pressure. Since I met him, he has taken medication for it, but every time he would go to the doctor for a checkup, or whatever else, the doctors would always say,

"Your blood pressure is high. You need to go check that out."

He never listened. Until one day, when he visited the cardiologist after work. While he was there, I received an urgent call informing me that Oscar had sustained a silent heart attack. I was seized by dread thinking this occurred while at the consultation. That was not the case. The doctor determined that when he did an EKG, he noticed Oscar had suffered a heart attack at some point in the previous days. He stressed to take him to the hospital to perform a catheterization. My body felt paralyzed with nausea at the thought of Oscar experiencing a heart attack alone, and we never realized it. I was holding on from exploding with sadness and fear or letting out a scream, not sure which, but maybe all of it at the same time. The only thing I knew about heart attacks was that they were deadly. I could feel my own arms wrapping around my torso and I was confused why I was involuntarily doing this, until I realized I was shaking. My body was prophesying.

When Oscar arrived home after leaving the doctor's office, he patiently made himself some food, ate, and showered, all in a deafening silence, while I gathered myself and some of his clothes to head to Baptist Hospital. The next day, they performed the catheterization, and when the doctor came out, I asked him,

"How is it? What did you find?"

He responded,

"Madame, your husband is a candidate for a heart transplant."

The air vaporized from my lungs. I was left stunned and had no idea how to respond other than,

"It can't be true."

He emphasized,

"It most certainly is. His heart is extremely damaged and he needs a transplant."

You can imagine the global impact that diagnosis caused in our lives, like an atomic bomb dropped. When I was finally allowed to see Oscar in his room, I shared the news as he stared at me repeating,

"I am not going to have a heart transplant. If my heart is bad, let it hang on until it wants. I am not going to live the last days of my life limited."

181

Darma, Oscar's mom, who was there at the time, interjected,

"We can get another opinion because maybe it isn't as bad as this doctor is saying."

We then requested for another renowned cardiologist to come and give an evaluation. The new cardiologist came to his room that afternoon and said,

"Yes, I reviewed everything and your heart is very weak with a 35% ejection fraction. The diagnosis is correct."

Oscar doubtfully inquired,

"Doctor, if I don't get the operation how many years of life do I have?"

The doctor, slow and precise, quoted:

"If you take care of yourself, abstain from eating meat, stop smoking, and create a clean lifestyle, you might have ten years, if not five."

I wanted a better answer, I needed Oscar to stick around. I needed for him to be healthy. After that moment, our cyclical nightmare began.

Oscar made non-impactful life-saving changes to his routine. It wasn't for lack of trying, he just found it very difficult to abstain from all he liked. He would sneak a cigarette smoke when he could, continued eating meat and whatever he wanted, and partook in other habits not conducive to his state, and his friends who knew failed at helping him (yet they tried). Life continued with him, as if nothing had happened, as if he would have years to live, until about two years later. One night, while we were playing Dominoes with our usual crew on a Friday night, he got up from the table, with no hint at what was going on with him, to go to the bathroom. I remember him taking longer than usual in the bathroom. I decided to find out what was taking him so long. When I knocked at the door and asked how it was going, he said,

"I don't feel well."

I immediately pushed open the door and asked him

"What are you feeling?"

At this time, my heart was beating uncontrollably as I knew what was happening and he replied,

"I have a pain between my chest and my back."

I tried to keep my cool and calmly asked,

"Do you want me to tell the people to go?"

He muttered, trying to diffuse the situation

"No."

We had music playing in the background, as we did every Friday, and I casually exited the bathroom, went towards the radio, turned it off and addressed our guests as calmly as possible,

"Hey everyone, Oscar is not feeling good. I'm going to turn off the music, but if you want to leave and call it a night you can. I don't think he is able to keep playing."

While still in the bathroom, Oscar requested a BC powder, which was aspirin in powder form, which he would place under his tongue and drink to feel better. He did this on a routine basis when he felt bad. I gave him the powder and he downed it with water. I met his eyes and felt the pain he was in, not just physically, but emotionally, as we both knew and feared what would happen next.

Zule, my best friend, who was a nurse (and was also there with us) began to worry. She entered the bedroom where Oscar was now sitting on our bed, and asked to take his blood pressure. Although still worried, she reassured us his pulse was good. Oscar was still feeling unwell. His beautiful eyes were watery, and his skin was as pale as a ghost. I asked him,

"Please tell me what you want me to do because I see you a little pale. Do you want me to call for a rescue?"

The first time he said,

"No."

But a little while later he stressed,

"Call me an ambulance."

I immediately called and Oscar went to the living room and sat on the sofa to patiently wait for them. Most of the people we had over had left, except Pac (a sweet caring man who was one of his friends) and Zule, who stayed to see if I needed help. She understood my pain and I loved her dearly for it. She was my dearest friend and has been through various hardships with me. Every second stretched to an eternity —sitting there with all my thoughts, praying he would be ok, hoping it was nothing. When they arrived, they told him he was, in fact, having a *heart attack*. There it was, my worst fear. I lost it, even though I tried holding it together for Oscar's sake, for my sake, and for everyone's sake. I prayed, not today, God, let him stay with us. Please, not today.

They took him that night to Pan American Hospital. When he arrived at the hospital, he was as if nothing was happening…making jokes, as always, typical Oscar. Meanwhile, secretly, I was in despair. The doctors treated him, doing everything they could until they decided to transfer him to Baptist Hospital the next day because they wanted to repeat the catheterization. They repeated the procedure and again informed him he would need an operation to unclog his arteries, which were severely blocked at this point. I was hoping this time he would pay attention and listen to them, but unfortunately, similar to last time, he said he would not do any surgery and that he would continue as he was. I reluctantly told him the final decision was his, that if he wanted to live a few more years and enjoy his life, he needed to take the doctor's recommendation. Looking back at the moment, I regret not pressuring him to do it. There was even a heart specialist and friend of the family, Dr. Daniel, who also strongly suggested he do the surgery. Oscar sternly responded,

"At this point, I am not ready for that."

I wonder what Oscar was thinking at the time. Was he scared? Did he want to die already? As I ponder thoughts about that moment, tears stream down my face, and I gasp for air to somehow find answers to why this happened. I will never heal from this, from loving Oscar. I hope to understand the meaning of it all one day. I thought of my grandkids, their joy was Oscar. I thought of my daughter who loved him as if he were her dad, and then I thought of me…all alone, living life without him. Me, a body with a heart half-beating.

That horrible heart attack was the second one he experienced. A year and a half later, or maybe two, the nightmare returned. I was at the hospital visiting my mother, who was admitted for something or other, when I received the call I dreaded. It was Oscar.

"Will you be long?"

I replied,

"Well, I'm here with Mami at the hospital. What is wrong?"

Again, he uttered the words I feared,

"I'm not feeling well."

Till today, when someone starts with,

"*I'm not feeling well.*" I lose the air, and my lungs collapse.

I asked,

"*Is your chest hurting?*"

He spoke softly,

"*Yes.*"

I kept on,

"*Does your jaw hurt?*"

He feared responding,

"*Yes,*"

I maintained focused,

"*Do you want me to call the rescue, because you are having a heart attack.*"

He sounded frightened,

"*No, just come home.*"

I hung up the phone, kissed my mother goodbye, and flew mindlessly through the streets of Miami. By the time I arrived home, Oscar was sitting in our trusty brown recliner, dressed and waiting for me. All I could think of was, what was he thinking of? What was going through his mind? Did he know? I was dead inside and only longed to help him. Once more, we gathered his things and raced through the streets to make it to the hospital. He, as always, with his jokes and mockeries,

"*Hey, If I don't die from a heart attack, you are going to kill me with your driving. Slow down, because I will make it.*"

He was so sure of himself, as if God told him he would survive this time. My heart melts every time I think about him and what he was internally going through, and at that moment, I knew I had to be strong for him, for us, and for our family.

Once we arrived at Baptist Hospital, they confirmed he was, in fact, having his third heart attack. The doctor that attended him said,

"It's now time to get operated on. If you don't, I'm not sure how long you have to live."

Again, as before, he was quite indecisive, and I had to speak with him, as his mother did too. Everyone spoke with him, recommending,

"Oscar, if you have the operation, it might extend your life, but if you don't you have no clue how long you'll live. Think about it."

I never wanted to pressure him to do anything because I didn't want if something did happen to live with my conscience knowing he did it because of me. I always waited for him to make his own decisions, hoping they were the right ones. He considered it, thought about it, and finally said yes, he would do the operation. I think back and wonder, what if he didn't have the operation? Would he have survived? Did I let him make the right choice? I struggled for many years with this until one day, I found peace as if Oscar came down from heaven and assured me everything was as it should be, and he was happy, and I was happy, even though I carry what feels like a shotgun-sized wound within me. I was born in pain and knew my life would be spent learning how to disguise and endure it.

Oscar's operation was on the 5th day of May 2001, a day I'll remember for the rest of my life. Waiting outside the operating room, praying he would survive, only to be told all went well, or we thought it did. He recovered and showed signs he was in good shape. Did he secretly know he was not good? Did he feel death knocking at his door? We pushed all that aside and continued with our lives. Once he completed his surgery and treatments, he, in fact, committed to living a healthy lifestyle and quit smoking. He did try to eat a bit healthier, but it made him miserable, not to be able to splurge on eating his favorites, but he stuck it out, for the most part. The Oscar that emerged from that surgery was different. He looked thin, tired, and humbled. Overall, he looked good, but internally, he wasn't. His lust for life diminished. He began to slowly, secretly die within.

All was well with us. The previous year, we had reserved a week-long vacation in Punta Cana for the end of July, beginning of August. When the day came to prepare for our vacation, we went to the cardiologist who performed the surgery and informed him that we had this vacation planned over a year ago and wanted to know if he could go. The cardiologist assured us that yes, we could. He felt Oscar was doing well and could travel. He said,

"Take with you this last result of his electrocardiogram just in case, so you could have it with you."

He gave me the report. We left for our vacation with Angelica and Pac (Angelica was Pac's wife) to Punta Cana. I remember thinking life was nice, until I would look into Oscar's eyes and feel a chill of doom, which I could not explain. As if something horribly unforeseen was in the air. Something he couldn't find the will to speak of, nor I wanted to hear.

We were in Punta Cana for a week, trying our best to enjoy the moment and the time together. Oscar drank and ate well throughout the trip, but he couldn't stay up late due to his weakened state. He just wanted to relax. I wonder if he was contemplating life—life without him, life without the kids or me. When night came around, he would tell me in his gentle way that he was tired. His legs were hurting, and his energy was low. Of course, I thought to myself, he just had a major surgery prior, so it was logical that he felt that way. We never realized the worst, never imagined the outcome, nor our delicate reality. Within those moments, we truly had a wonderful time. We drank, we laughed, went to the pool, beach, and enjoyed ourselves, but always with a looming essence of him knowing he was not well, of all of us knowing Oscar's time was running low. His battery was expiring.

Oscar (Pa) (El Buey)

During the entire trip, Oscar would call Huston daily without fail. There wasn't a single day that would pass wherein he wouldn't go to the lobby and request a call to Miami. As everyone knew, Oscar adored Dalton and Nikki, but Huston was Oscar's obsession. His love for Huston was pure and ancient. They had the kind of connection that felt karmic Something we could only bear witness to and wonder what sort of lives those two have spent together before. Sometimes, we thought they were one soul in separate bodies. He left for that vacation, all the while wanting to take Huston with us. Unfortunately, that wasn't possible, due to various reasons, which he terribly regretted. I wish today we would have taken Huston with us and given them a beautiful parting gift of being with each other before having to say one last goodbye.

We returned to Miami on August 5th, wherein at the airport, Kelly and Huston were enthusiastically waiting for him. I will never forget the hug Oscar and Huston shared when they saw each other at the airport and that enduring love in their eyes. It made me weep. They embraced with deep love for each other, a love we all need. Maybe it was that Huston healed something in him, as if he saw Oscar as the man Oscar always wanted to be.

On a footnote, I must say that Pac and Angelica, who were with us when we arrived at the airport, commented to me that the last time Angelica and he saw Oscar was that day at the airport, hugging Huston. It was the most beautiful display of love they had ever seen.

Oscar's Last Day

Living in Florida may teach you how to handle a hurricane—but there are some storms in life you cannot weather. We had returned from Santo Domingo on a Sunday, and the next weekend, Huston had a baseball tournament in West Palm Beach. As you recall, at that time I had the clinic, and his first game was going to be on Friday afternoon, followed by a game on Saturday and Sunday as well. Knowing I had to work on Saturday, since I was just on vacation the week prior, I organized appointments with patients for the doctor to visit them, making it impossible to leave until Saturday midday. Oscar wanted to leave on Friday, and instead of leaving with only Huston, he said,

"I'm going to take all three kids."

No matter the mystical connection with Huston, he had his own lovely magic with Dalton and Nikki as well. A heart that big proved a bottomless ocean of pure love. Those kids were his three miracles. He adored them, even more so than me, their grandmother, which I didn't know was possible. I imagine, since he wasn't close to his own child, not a fault of his, he loved being close to Kelly's kids. They became the children he never had the opportunity to enjoy. Oscar, Huston, Dalton and Nikki were glued to each other. Oscar's only child was born with a physical defect, causing his first years to be quite difficult. It felt, to me, as if Oscar secretly longed to have a father-son relationship with his child, without it being poisoned by his ex-wife. When my grandkids were born, he adopted those kids as his; he loved, cared, and did everything for them. He helped raise them, fed them, cared for them, taught them how to play baseball, ride bikes, go-karts, golf, and most importantly he showed them love. He called Huston *"Choo Choo"* Dalton, *"Dalty"*, and Nikki *"Nicks"*, I was "Mama", and he was "Pa".

191

He repeated,

"I'm going to take all three kids with me."

I responded,

"Are you crazy? How are you going to go with three kids?"

There was no way I could deter him from taking them with him. I wonder if Oscar felt this would be his last weekend with them. We spoke with Charly, the father of the kids, and planned that he would pick me up when I finished at the clinic, and we would head on directly to the baseball game. Oscar hadn't been working for seven months since the surgery due to his condition, so the financial weight rested on the support of my clinic. When he arrived at West Palm Beach he called me for help checking into the hotel that the other coaches and parents were staying at. He felt embarrassed asking since it was an expensive option.

"I'm looking for a hotel, but they are quite far, and everyone is stay-ing at the Hilton (or the Marriott, I don't quite remember)*, so if you don't mind, let's rent there."*

I happily agreed,

"No problem Oscar, use the card and rent where everyone is staying."

That is what he did. Thank God we made that decision. I would have given him the world if he asked me.

He spent the entire day on Friday with Huston, Dalton, and Nikki at the game. He joked, ran around, and played baseball with the kids all afternoon. I'm certain he loved every moment of that day. On Saturday, as planned, Charly picked me up, and we went directly to the park where the game was in progress. It was terribly hot in the month of August. When we arrived, Oscar was there, sweating, looking pale and tired. He told me,

"I didn't sleep much. Dalton was snoring and I was tossing and turning all night."

I told him,

"Why don't you go to the hotel and we'll stay here at the game until it's done? We'll take the kids there once it's over. You can rest."

He said,

"No, I'm staying here until the game finishes."

What would have happened if I urged him to go and lay down? Would he have lapsed into a forever sleep and left us all without a last I love you?

There he stayed, as always, saying his jokes, talking to everyone, until the game finished. Oscar was loved by so many. Everyone dreams to be loved like that, unconditionally and forever. When the game finished, we all went back to the hotel, not knowing what was to come. Not realizing that was the last baseball game he would spend with the kids.

One of the kids that played with Huston on the team, Drew, his father had gone to see the game, but he was not staying at the hotel, he was leaving back to Miami, Drew wanted to stay in the room with us if we didn't mind, so he wouldn't have to go back with his dad. We decided for him to stay with us. That afternoon, when we returned from the baseball game, all the kids wanted to go to the pool. We all went to the pool, including Oscar. Although I wanted him to stay in the room to relax, he did not want to. He went and played in the pool with the kids, doing silly things like putting Huston on his shoulders to play chicken in the water. He didn't stop. The pool games were over, and we went up to our room. Everyone bathed and dressed, and the entire group was going to go to eat at Flanigan's, a trendy sports bar & grill. We all went, including Charly, who was leaving after eating because he needed to go to work the next day, since it was Sunday. The entire group went, including the coaches, wives, kids, and us. We all sat at a big table. Oscar didn't have much of an appetite, something that struck me strange, because he always ate well. He ate a salad and some little bits here and there. When dessert came around, he said,

"I want a carrot cake."

I immediately thought that he shouldn't eat it because it has tons of grease. But at that moment, I thought, what the hell, let him eat his carrot cake. He ate his carrot cake, his late carrot cake in pure delight.

We returned to the hotel, and when we were getting ready for bed, there were two beds and an air mattress. He told me,

"I want to sleep on the floor on the air mattress alone, since last night I didn't get to sleep. I need to rest."

I responded,

"No worries."

I slept with Nikki, Huston, and Dalton in the other bed. Drew slept on the floor, in between both beds, where we had laid a sheet and some pillows. Oscar slept on the air mattress. We were all in bed, ready to sleep, extremely tired of the day, when Oscar passed by Drew and farted by him, typical Oscar. Everyone died of laughter as Drew chimed with laughter that the fart was super smelly. Oscar then stood in the middle of the room and said,

"I'm going to lay down because, se me esta acabando la bateria."

(that was a private joke he shared with the kids and myself) [translation: My batteries are dying.] We all went to bed.

The night before, since there was going to be a game in the morning and then after the game we were planning to leave back to Miami, I left all the luggage packed and ready, left Huston's uniform out, and everything ready so that when we got up early, we could just go to the park and leave.

Around 5:00/5:30 a.m., I was awakened by Oscar's constant coughing. It was a sound I often heard on some nights and thought nothing of it, but tonight's cough sent me to check on him, but he wasn't in bed, he was in the bathroom. The hairs all over my body raised as if I was struck by lightning. I heard him continue coughing and coughing. With every cough, I worried more and more. I found myself asking him,

"What is happening to you?"

He was breathless, all the while still coughing, and looked at me, unable to speak. My heart was pounding when I asked,

"Does your chest hurt?"

He motioned with his head,

"No."

The doctor had prescribed him a nitroglycerin pill, which he had in a locket around his neck. In case he ever felt chest pain, he could put it under his tongue and it would help him. When I saw him breathless, I locked eyes with him and noticed the scared look in his eyes. My body began to tremble as he struggled to speak, and I quickly grabbed opened the locket secretly surrounding his neck and put the glycerin pill in his mouth under his tongue. This commotion caused Huston and Nikki to wake, both as in unison, rubbing their sleepy eyes open sluggishly, asked

"Pa, are you ok?"

Barely able to speak but using every strength he had left within him as if he was stealing his last breath, Oscar mustered to whisper,

"I'm fine."

Those were the last words Oscar said to them.

Oscar's expression, which had been seared into my soul, alerted me that he was not well. I immediately called the lobby and asked the receptionist if she could call the rescue. I urgently exited the hallway and knocked on the coach's room, which was situated next to our room. I, as calmly as I could, explained I had called the rescue because Oscar was not feeling well. I hoped that since the kids were sleeping, he could stay with the kids while I went to the hospital with Oscar. He, without a second thought, said,

"No problem."

He and his wife came out of their room and kindly waited in the hallway with us until the rescue team arrived. Oscar slowly, almost staggering, walked out to the hallway to lay down on the stretcher waiting for him. The rescuers immediately began administering oxygen to Oscar. They performed their routine checkup in matters such as these and shared that Oscar was suffering from congestive heart failure. I turned to Oscar and assured him he would be fine, explaining,

"That is exactly what my mom and dad had a few weeks back, and they were ok afterward."

I wanted to give Oscar some sort of peace at that moment, finding some solemnity for him to relax and be tranquil, as long as possible. I was dying inside. I wanted to scream.

While in the middle of the hallway with the front door of our room still open, Oscar signaled with his eyes for me to close the door. At first, I didn't understand what he was trying to tell me. I was not certain whether he wanted me to call the kids or Huston. That's when I decided to ask him,

"Do you want me to call Huston?"

196

He signaled no with his head. The coach's wife said,

"I think he wants you to close the door."

Exactly that, he did not want the kids, if they were up to see him in the stretcher with the oxygen mask on. I told the Coach's wife,

"I'm going with him in the ambulance, and if I don't return from the hospital before the baseball game, please take the kids to the park. I have all our luggage ready, can you put them in the car?"

She understood,

"No problem, you can leave peacefully knowing we will take care of the kids."

I climbed in the ambulance with Oscar and was praying during the entire trip, asking God for nothing bad to happen to him. I was praying so hard, I felt myself vibrating, as if I would levitate from the floor. There was a moment before we arrived at the hospital when I noticed the ambulance had slowed down. That worried me a bit, but I was always hoping everything was good. When we arrived at the hospital, I tried to jump out of the ambulance, but the medic held me by the arm and asked me to wait until they brought Oscar out and attended to him first, and then I could go in. I stayed sitting there motionless, imagining we were home in bed, side by side, watching our favorite show, as they rolled him down towards the emergency room. The hospital in West Palm Beach was quite small, and outside the ER, there was a large glass window where you could see the room where they brought Oscar. When I hopped out of the ambulance, as if I was watching a movie, a group of doctors and nurses rushed around the stretcher and it looked as if one of the nurses who was facing me was smiling. At the moment, a peaceful feeling engulfed me, thinking Oscar was with his jokes again. I then remembered I had his EKG report that the cardiologist had given me in my purse, so I frantically told the medic from the rescue who was still there,

"I could give it to the doctor."

The paramedic looked at me and said,

"Do you need a hug?"

Confused, I replied, as if whispering,

"Yes."

He hugged me, which took me by surprise, because of everything going on around us at the time, but I did not make anything out of it. Later on, I realized the meaning of the gesture.

At this point, I was moving on reflex, sat down to register Oscar, and as I was there, giving them all the details, I could see behind her through the glass window, still the emergency room. The doctor came out to where I was, and I asked him,

"How is he, doctor?"

He quickly responded,

"We are doing everything we can, but it does not look good. If you have more family, call them."

At that moment, as you can imagine, my blood went cold, even though I was still hoping nothing was going to happen. I continued as if I became a robot just giving the information to the clerk. When I heard the famous—

"Code Blue—Code Blue"

At that point, I started losing hope. Fear, confusion, and anger rose within me, but I had to keep it together. I immediately started calling Kelly, but Kelly didn't pick up. She must have been sleeping, she mentioned she was going out the previous night and would get home late. I called Oscar's brother, Juan, instead of his mother, who I did not want to call until we knew more. I called Juan and said,

"Your brother is in the hospital. Apparently, things don't look good. If you want to come, call your mother, speak with her, and come."

He said,

"Ok."

I tried calling Kelly again, but she did not pick up. I thought to call Charly, who was on his way to work when I called. I said,

"Charly, I'm here at the hospital with Oscar and things don't look good. I don't know what to do. I'm alone and the kids are at the hotel."

He said,

"Don't worry, I'm going to call work and go directly to where you are."

I called Carlos, Kelly's father, to see if he knew where Kelly was and to see if he could locate her. I told him about the situation that I was going through.

He lovingly asked,

"Do you want me to come?"

Working off of reflex, I blurted,

"No, Charly is going to come, and I've called Oscar's brother and mother. Don't worry."

199

While that was happening, the doctor came out, and when I saw his face, I knew what he was going to tell me.

He sadly spoke,

"We couldn't do anything."

My world immediately fell apart, crumbling my faith and hopes, losing the man I loved. I felt faint. I asked if I could see him. They responded,

"We are preparing him. When he is ready, I will let you know so you can see him."

I grabbed the phone and noticed my fingers shivering, trying to force my hands to cooperate. I needed to make calls, first calling his brother,

"Don't come. Oscar is dead. Tell your mother."

Tears streamed down my wet blouse. I then called Charly, who was on his way, and managed to say something:

"Charly, Oscar has just died."

Charly started crying and crying, sobbing like I've never heard a grown man cry. I tried consoling him. I tried consoling me. I tried consoling us.

"Stop driving, pull over, and calm down so you don't have an accident."

I called the coach and gave him the horrible news. Shocked, he asked me,

"What do you want me to do with the kids?"

I responded as calm as possible,

"If you can, please bring them to the hospital."

He later said to me that when he went back to the room and told the kids they were going to the hospital, Huston simply asked,

"Should I put on my uniform for the game?"

He held tears while he replied,

"Yes, put it on."

All the air I had within me evaporated, and I was left a hollow shell as he told me this. The coach didn't know what to say to Huston. Huston proudly changed into his baseball uniform, joined his brother and sister, and headed toward the hospital. That was, I can truly say, the toughest day of my life— the *worst* day of my life. When the kids got off the car, I was outside waiting for them. They came, and all three of them, without knowing anything that had occurred, stood in front of me. I hugged them, and the only thing I could do was say,

"Pa's dead."

As I stood there, numb from shock, staring into my grandkid's eyes, I only managed to add more pain when I asked them if they wanted to see Oscar one last time. In my mind, all I thought about was,

"What if one day they would regret not seeing him for the last time?"

But immediately, Huston uttered firmly for all of them,

"No."

I heard myself let out a sigh of relief, for I too longed that they would remember Oscar as he was in the pool playing with them after a fun baseball game. While lost in that moment, the coach tugged me to the side and wondered what to do with the kids. I informed him Charly was en route. It pained me to ask another hurtful question to Huston, as he was still a child who just lost his best friend and grandpa. But, there I was,

"Huston, do you want to stay here to wait for your dad, or do you want to go play baseball?"

It was his last game. He paused thought for a second, and then blurted out,

"No, mama, I'm going to play baseball because that is what Pa would have wanted me to do."

The kids have called Oscar *"Pa"* since the day they were born. That day I felt Huston's heartbreak. He and his broken heart left to play that last baseball game without Oscar, without his Pa, I was gutted. The coach shared with me afterward that when they arrived at the park, he relayed to everyone what had happened. There was not a single person who didn't cry over the news. Oscar was infinitely beloved by the kids, the parents, the coaches…everybody. I believe they all played that game with broken hearts. Sadly, they didn't win, all because their hearts weren't on the game that day, they were with Oscar. I can only imagine it was one of the saddest and most difficult days for my grandkids, especially for Huston, who went on to play his game, knowing his Pa would never see another of his games again.

Nikki and Dalton stayed with me, waiting for Charly to arrive. They didn't quite understand the gravity of the events that played out with Oscar. I often wondered if this traumatic experience for them so young would scar them for life. I decided at that moment that Oscar's memory would be the loveliest one of all. When Charly arrived, who looked as if he had been continuously crying, I immediately went into motion and started making all the arrangements. I had to call Oscar's cardiologist to inform him to submit the death certificate. I can honestly say that return car ride with Charly, Dalton, and Nikki, as Oscar's car stayed in the lot waiting for the coach, who did me a favor to drive it to Miami, that car trip, those two to three hours, was one of the most horrible trips of my life, all the while thinking I had left Oscar dead in West Palm Beach and that he would never return to his house. Tears streamed down my blouse. Screams spat out of my mouth, uncontrollable utter screams with Charly desperately trying to keep it together himself and the kids in the back seat, wailing as well, unaware of what to do with all the feelings in the car. Aside from everything, I had no plans on what to do, as we hadn't prepared for this, although we imagined Oscar's days had been numbered, he never wanted to make funeral arrangements. He didn't care about stuff like that. On the car trip, I continued with the calls to those closest and communicated the sad news. Everyone was in shock, although they expected something, it was not anticipated, especially for me.

A part of me somewhat felt Oscar was secretly ill, scaring me to imagine he could die at any moment, but I never let that thought in my mind, or how I was going to feel when it happened. I pushed those ugly thoughts away from my existence.

When we arrived at the house in Miami, Carlos, my first husband and the father of my kids were waiting for me outside. That was what a grand quality that man had, that was his character. He hugged me and softly whispered,

"Don't be sad. I just saw him, and he said he was good, that he isn't suffering anymore. He is good."

Those words hugged my heart and gave my soul faith. I felt Oscar's love at that moment and have been till today.

Allow me the time to insert a small note at this point, amidst all the pain, disheartening, and crying, when there always lies something coherent. While in the car traveling back, I thought it important to get a better understanding of Nikki's and Dalton's recollection of the entire trip. My mind rattled with the notion of how traumatic and sad for both of them, only being ten and eleven, this event has left them. I looked back at them as they cried. I believe it was mainly because they saw me crying, screaming with desperation from not accepting what had happened. Nikki leans over to Dalton, as she is frantically crying, and asks,

"Dalton, you're not crying?"

Dalton innocently responded,

"Nikki, I already cried ten napkins."

That comment made me laugh, and it's something I remember till today. At that moment, I felt a strange calmness and tranquility come over me.

Shortly after arriving home, the friends started piling in, the people who, in fact, truly loved him. All of Oscar's friends from baseball and Dominoes night had arrived, Pac, Miguel, El Magnifico, Robert, all of them came; Zule came, all of them kept coming to fill in the house to honor Oscar *"El Buey"* PA. These big, burly, strong men cried like little babies. We all knew Oscar was ill, and at any given moment, he could leave us, but it was still an unexpected departure, one that left a hole in all our hearts. After Oscar had the surgery, he looked better, and we all thought that surgery would extend his life at least five to ten more years. Unfortunately, it didn't.

That day with our friends and family, Kelly finally arrived. I believe it was Lisset, Yayi's daughter, who delivered the dreaded news. When Kelly entered and saw me, she looked destroyed, almost fainting in the hallway of our house. She was truly not accepting of the situation. She was in utter shock, much like the rest of us. She painfully regretted not being able to answer my call, but life sometimes shields you from experiencing more pain at once; it only gives you what you can take, and having to tell Kelly Pa died would have been the straw on the camel's back. I would have lost it. I heard from Lisset that

204

after she told Kelly, Kelly let out a primal scream that she will forever remember. It sent daggers down her spine. I'm grateful God saved me from delivering that news, not sure I could have taken any more pain.

It was time to start the grueling task of looking into how we would bury and mourn Oscar. As I mentioned, I had nothing planned, but my stepfather, Antonio, who had a heart of gold and the kindest man I've ever known, arrived at the house and said,

"Clara, you can use the plot we have paid for us. Use it and then we will see how it gets worked out."

He gave me the option not to advance any money at that time, firstly, because I didn't have it, and secondly, because it was too quick. I went to the cemetery with him and completed the transfer. I went to the funeral to choose a casket for Oscar. One never thinks of or talks about what kind of casket one favors. My mind was at a baseball game with Oscar, not thinking about caskets, but in the end, I found one. One that I feel he would have liked. The process continued in arranging the viewing and the painful burial.

When I called my son, he promptly came and stayed with me during those first painful days, giving me much-needed moral support.

It pains me to share that Oscar's family, as I remember, did not lend a hand at the funeral. They failed to lend a hand throughout the entire process. But regardless, those matters at the time weren't important, what was important was that Oscar's mother was left destroyed. She never imagined losing her son, and it was an extremely hard jolt for her and for Joe (his dad) as well, because he adored Oscar. But as we all know, life continues.

When the neighbors started noticing all the people and commotion at our house, as there was a big group of people everywhere, someone came, I don't recall which of our neighbors it was, that came over to see what was happening. When they heard of Oscar's death, the entire neighborhood mourned. Everyone in that neighborhood adored Oscar, even the kids, because Oscar was one of them, he was a kid at heart. Andy, a sweet boy who lived across the street from our house and was like an adopted grandkid to us, told his father that he would give his right arm for Oscar to return (Andy was a right-handed pitcher in baseball and the kids' best friend). The love I witnessed from Andy for Oscar was truly a beautiful thing. Everyone's love of Oscar made me miss him even more. That night, before Andy went to bed, he wrote a letter to Oscar and put it in his shoe. I can see his sad face streaming with tears as he penned his last words to Oscar. A tiny pure gesture that reaches deeply into one's soul. I wonder what he wrote in the letter? Maybe one day I'll ask him.

Later at the funeral, I have to say, if you recall, my grandkids refused to go to the funeral. They did not want to see Oscar dead. The kids from baseball did go. Those kids cried rivers that night. They would hug me, and at that moment, I could feel the immense pain and suffering resonating from these sweet boys, and my soul ached upon watching them. Oscar was truly a beloved man. He would have never imagined what his death meant to so many people. His loss, we still feel it today. *Se le acabo la bateria.*

Oscar, wherever you are, please know you were extremely loved. You shall forever be remembered.

Life After Oscar

The months after Oscar's death were excruciating. The earth tore and swallowed me whole for months, only to begin again, practically from zero. In other words, here I was alone again, with the financial responsibility of the house and debt, which I incurred after Oscar died. At that time, I had a clinic, and it became difficult to manage the business and my new situation. I fell into a state of profound despair. For the first three months, I didn't have the will to open my eyes, let alone get up from bed. Days were filled with uncontrollable sobbing for hours, and while my mind disappeared from continuing with the clinic, I decided to sell it. Fortune shines its light on me because as soon as I spoke with the on-site doctor, I asked him if he knew anyone who would want to take over the clinic. To my surprise, he immediately found someone, and that person ended up staying in the office. I sold it and went home to cry. I've become an expert in that field. Crying for my kids, home, Oscar, and myself.

Three weeks after Oscar's passing, Huston had an important baseball tournament in Orlando. Let's remember that Oscar never missed Huston's games, and we originally planned on attending before Oscar's passing. Charlie ended up taking the three kids and myself. We stayed at a small hotel in Kissimmee, and attended the first game ever without Oscar. This was extremely painful, watching the game without Oscar. During the game, every time Huston went up to bat, I looked up at the sky and, secretly weeping, said: *Oscar, are you up there watching? Look at your boy, how good he is doing,* all the while knowing how devastating it was for Huston, who was playing his heart out without his Pa watching and cheering him on. Pa's absence now from their games would leave a profound scar on Dalton and Nikki as well. He coached, not only Huston, but Dalton and Nikki in the game he loved dearly. I wasn't a person who believed in signs, but when the game ended, and we were walking towards the exit to meet Huston, a young man who was involved in the organization, approached me. Mind you, there were a ton of people walking along with us. Charly was by my side and the kids were ahead of us. The young guy said to me,

"Lady, your husband said to tell you that he is up there."

I looked at him confused and answered,

"No, that message is not for me"

He kindly insisted and went on to share:

"Yes, he told me to let you know that he is upstairs, meaning up in the stand above the field."

I had to compose myself for fear I would burst out crying. Charly interrupted him explaining,

"No, that message is not for her, her husband passed away."

The man did not know how to react. He was embarrassed, but I said:

"No, it is ok. I know he is up there watching. Thank you."

After that, I began to believe in signs. That encounter was not the only one. My first gift to Oscar when we moved in together was a light brown double comfy recliner. We would sit and watch TV together, and when the grandkids came over, we would all squish together. One day, I walked in and saw Huston and Oscar sitting together, and I thought to take a picture of them. This became a ritual. I took pictures of Oscar and Huston throughout different stages of Huston's life.

Oscar and Huston on their favorite chair

After Oscar's passing, I decided to get a new sofa and dispose of the recliner, as it was agonizing sitting alone without him. I would sit there and remember all the good times we shared together while sitting on the recliner. After several trips to different furniture stores, one afternoon while at work, I asked my friend and coworker, Jude, to accompany me to Al's, my ex-brother-in-law's furniture store, to look at the sofas. That day, Al was not there, but his son Ian was. Ian was a big man with a kind heart. As soon as I got into the store, there was a sofa that caught my attention. It was a leather salmon-colored sofa. I looked over at Jude and signaled that it was the one. We walked over to the counter and asked the price, which, to our surprise, was quite affordable. I told him I found my new couch. He started preparing the invoice, and when he gave it to me to sign, I noticed the name Oscar written on the paper.

Confused, I asked him why was Oscar's name on the invoice, and he replied:

"Because that's the name of the model of that particular sofa."

I couldn't believe that while I came to replace Oscar's recliner, all the while holding a heavy heart and not sure if I should, God, in the process, was reinforcing the bond Oscar and I had with a sign that Oscar would always be in our lives. Tell me now how you don't believe in signs because now I do.

While in the deepest despair of my mourning, almost five months after Oscar's passing, my mother became quite ill and was admitted to the hospital. She had become extremely delicate, she wouldn't eat or attempt anything at all. My world, once more, was jolted. They admitted her with the intention to operate and ease her ailment. The operation was not successful. When she emerged from surgery there was a respiratory machine attached to her due to her weakened lungs. I was devastated, all the while thinking she would not survive this.

Grief had chosen a home within.

At that time, a friend offered me a job in her office. She owned a clinic and proposed that I work at her clinic to administer the office. I had my doubts, so I told her I couldn't do it under the circumstances. I had my mother in the hospital, and I was depressed because of Oscar's passing. She told me,

"Don't worry. Tell me the hours you want to work, tell me the day you want to come. Come in, do the work at your leisure, your way, however you need to do it, but I need you to come and organize my office."

I thought maybe this was what I needed to break out of my depression, so I accepted. My life started anew in that office a couple of hours a day and ended by visiting my mother in the hospital.

Sadly, my mother was four months in the hospital, never being able to get off the ventilator and breathe on her own. Coincidentally, my mother was in the hospital when my father was unexpectedly admitted to the hospital several times due to his Alzheimer's.

In the month of April, seven months after Oscar's passing, both my parents were patients in the same hospital; Lola, my mom, was on the fourth floor, and my Dad was on the third. Dad went in for some respiratory difficulties. Having both parents facing the end of life at the same time was more than I could handle, but God gave me the strength I needed when I needed it the most.

Fortunately, I was able to stay one night with my Dad and in the morning, I gave him his breakfast. He loved cheese and fruits in the morning, even though he didn't recognize me. Afterwards, he fell asleep while I recalled a story. I enjoyed those moments with him, not knowing they would be our last. I went home to get some rest. Later that day, his wife called me in shock, explaining Elias hadn't woken, and the doctors confirmed he was in a comatose state. In the late hours of that night, my father, Elias, moved on to another plane. His departure was very tranquil. He didn't suffer, something I am grateful for. God allowed me that special day with him to say goodbye. Aside from all the normal family dramas of ups and downs, he was a respectably good man; a man that loved me and took care of his family and helped tons of people throughout his life. A month later on May 17, my mother passed. They had both been born in the same year, a month apart, and they died the exact year a month apart, under the same roof—talk about coincidences.

The years between 2001 and 2002 were unbearable. In practically one year, I became a widow and an orphan. The death of my parents resonated a huge impact in my life, but the death of Oscar left a gaping hole in my heart, which would last years. Time doesn't wait around for you, it keeps ticking. Life continues. I just had to find my normal again, which, in my case, took two to three years for me to reenter society and adhere to a different life. My children, grandkids and friends were a huge support and the source of my wellbeing throughout the years.

Months after Oscar's passing, I began collecting a group of wonderful girlfriends who quickly became the center of my support. When I was married to Oscar, our friends were all males, who would come to play Dominoes every Friday. We had a handful of friends who were couples—one which was Robert (an extremely talented musician) and his wife, Zule (a nurse and the most amazing human). They would frequently join us at Dominoes' night and vacations. Robert and Oscar worked together at some point, much like Zule and I, who worked at the Travelers together. She was and is still today my longest and most trusted best friend throughout my life.

My support group friends Left to Right: Jacky, Ani, Me, Silvi, Zulema (Zule), Gladys

With time, I slowly started meeting other friends. I met Mercy, a fun-loving woman whom I had first encountered during my work at the Hialeah clinic. At the time she was the girlfriend of the doctor that worked in the clinic. We became fast friends, but the kind that you would only see at the office, sometimes at lunch. It wasn't until after Oscar passed that we reconnected and began a more social life as close friends. After meeting Mercy, Jackie entered my life, a wild blonde with a lust for living. I met Jackie, who was introduced to me by a common friend, Benitez. I had established the title company with my daughter by then, Clear Title of South Florida, and she owned a mortgage broker firm, which was a good working connection, enabling us to quickly become a great match. She became my second great friend. After Jackie, I met Gladys, a more serious woman, who had also recently become a widow. Let me mention that all of these women were widows: Mercy, Jackie, and Gladys—not that I planned on having widows as friends, it just happened organically. Lastly, there was Ani, my sweet, loving cousin, who, although she was married, would join in with us any time we had a reunion or occasion. Her husband Mandy was the coolest husband, taking her traveling all around the world. Ani worked with Kelly and myself at the title company. She was the referee between us and the one who kept tempers at a low when things would get heated with my daughter and I. We would have never made it without Ani. She was our right hand at Clear Title. Later, after Jackie, I met Sylvia, she was the funniest one in the group. Zule also joined the group occasionally, but nevertheless, my rock at all times. This group of women carried me through months of sorrow, until one day, about five years after Oscar's death, I casually met someone who I decided to date. This was something I never thought I would do again, but as I said, time keeps ticking and life keeps moving. That relationship went nowhere, as you could have imagined.

Clear Title Saved Us

Me at Clear Title of South Florida

In 2004, Kelly was working with a prestigious attorney at the time, specializing in transactional/corporate/real estate law. He trained Kelly enough wherein she felt she could venture on her own and she was exceptional at it. I remember the day when she approached me,

"Mom, why don't we start our own business?"

That question had us throwing ideas around, as she was unsure what kind of business to open. We started to ponder our options. She wanted a library or like a restaurant/café, not sure, but she had a few ideas in mind. We ultimately ended up with a title company since Kelly already had a profession in real estate.

Kelly assured me she could find clients, and since I most certainly liked the administration portion of a business, I said to her,

"Well, let's open an office. I'll administer it and you do the professional side."

After months of me searching for an office and her ability to resign from her position, which at the time allowed her a lucrative lifestyle (she left a good job for the possibility of being her own boss and making less), we finally christened the business in 2004. We rented a small office on Flagler Street and barely furnished it with some furniture my stepbrother, Jose, hand-crafted for us, with the rest of the equipment found at Goodwill. Since Ani, my favorite cousin, had recently been laid off from the insurance company she worked for, I spoke with her and she came on board to join our group. Kelly maintained working for the attorney (who was a total gentlemen with her departure— they are still in contact with each other till today) until we finished setting up the office. We started bringing in clients, and the business commenced a wonderful path, a new beginning in life again. I loved working with my daughter and cousin, but our personalities often clashed.

Clear Title went through highs and lows. The highs having an enormous amount of business due to the housing market blowing up in 2006. We were having about five closings a day some days, and others, we were dealing with the chaos of the market. Clear Title allowed my daughter, Kelly, to gift me with the car of my dreams, a Mercedes-Benz. I owned this car until we moved out of Miami.

The Boatman

In 2005, I re-encountered Ral, a long-haired, good-natured hippie who had worked with me at the insurance company when I was the supervisor of the personal injury department at Latin America Insurance. He had resigned some years later to work for a big company, Allstate, causing me to lose contact with him. He would randomly pass by my house, but we really didn't have much contact other than an occasional outing. When he learned of Oscar's passing, he called me to express his condolences. One day, he overheard that we had opened a title company, coincidently a block from where he worked at Allstate. He randomly showed up at the office and offered to take Ani (her child-like wonder and sweet disposition were truly angelic) and I went out to lunch. Afterwards, we enjoyed speaking routinely, until he casually invited me out to dinner. I accepted, not thinking much about it, then he poured out his heart and confessed he was always in love with me. He asked if we could be friends first and then see if we could develop a relationship of some sort. That is what we did, since I wasn't ready for anything else, and I did miss having a companion, we decided to have a go at it.

I decided to see where it led with Ral, although he was a bit eccentric, he was well educated, with good manners, and a decent, hard worker who cared for me dearly. In those days, I knew Ral loved me more than I did him, after all I was still in love with Oscar. He took care of me emotionally and was extremely genuine and gentle with me. Unfortunately, being with him didn't last, and thus, we had a relatively short relationship. In my head, the reason for dating him was my need for someone decent and honest to help me through my loneliness. Maybe that reason was selfish, and when I decided to break things off, he reacted like a gentleman, understanding me while

216

still loving me. I'll always carry reverence for Ral and his soft demeanor. We remained good friends. I last heard he bought a boat to travel the world, which is what he always wanted to do. I'm happy for him. His relationship came at a point in my life where I needed his grounded energy, which helped plant me back into Earth.

The French Man

Not long after I ended my relationship with Waldo, I decided to take some time off for myself to recover from those five intense years. I did enjoy and loved the time spent having fun; it kept my mind busy and far from thinking about Oscar. I actually liked the romance of our relationship, not rationalizing it in any way, just simply living life without the responsibility of giving an account to this man of my life. The free space allowed me to have a life with my girlfriends again, spend time with my family, and enjoy my freedom. More importantly, after it was over, I wanted to spend time with myself.

Meanwhile, one day, while I was playing FarmVille and CityVille on my computer (don't judge, it's fun), one of the players sent me a friendly message. I replied just as friendly. It turns out he was a single older French man who lived in a small, obscure town in France and who also loved playing computer games. We began to communicate online about the game, then slowly bled into the intimacy realm. We questioned each other about our lives, all the while knowing this man did not know how to speak English, and I didn't speak French. We would communicate with the messages through the game, as it would translate for us. Life has a way of finding a way...

One day, he requested to see me through Skype, being that FaceTime didn't exist. He said,

"Let's Skype to meet each other."

I eagerly answered

"OK".

We scheduled a Skype session and finally introduced ourselves officially. The moment I saw him, I liked him. He was quite attractive, having a full head of white hair, sexy thin lips, and a beautiful spark about him. He was indeed an extremely charismatic French man. We continued our talks and learned our feelings were mutual. After months of communicating, we decided to meet in person, proposing I fly to Europe to meet him; quite adventurous and spontaneous, I accepted. But thought, who was I accepting a stranger's invitation to another country? Was I that desperate for affection? By the way, it didn't happen within two days, it was months, almost a year, actually, when we made plans to meet in March 2012 in Madrid, Spain. It was his courtesy to propose we meet in Madrid, that way I could speak my language if I had to, instead of flying to France, where it'll be difficult for me to understand, and it was easier for me to fly to Madrid from the United States. He was a sweet gentleman.

We made our plans and reserved our flights for the month of March. I found a hotel in Madrid and reserved two rooms, as I stressed we should have separate rooms. I wasn't sure if, after we met personally, we would still like each other or would want to stay together. I also wanted to be safe. I arranged to meet as friends, him in his room and me in mine. He agreed to everything. He shared his life story with me, stating he had a son and was divorced. His son had a girlfriend that was pregnant and was due to give birth precisely in the month of March. He, in turn, knew about my kids, grandkids, and friends. I introduced him to my Dominoes group, my friends, who would greet him in French. Everyone knew about my online relationship with the French man and that I was meeting him in March. Everyone was happy for me. They longed for me to be happy.

About three weeks prior to the trip, wherein I was practically packed and ready to go, he went silent. I began to get suspicious since we would normally communicate every day, either through computer or phone. I also noticed he wasn't playing the game or was active on the computer, making me extremely worried by then. One morning, quite early, I received a phone call from his son, who spoke broken English, struggling to inform me that his father was admitted to the hospital for a serious problem with his pancreas. He continued to explain that his father was unable to contact me due to his illness. I've often wondered what his son thought of me or if he even knew of me before that moment. And here he was on the phone, sharing that his father had requested him to call me and explain what was going on and to postpone the trip because his father wasn't in any shape to travel. I let him know it wasn't a problem and to tell him to call me when he was better. I canceled the trip, leaving myself let down, again, by life. A sign from the universe keeping me single and on my own. But I reminded myself, when one door closes, God has another one ready to be opened.

I believe it was during that week that his son's girlfriend gave birth to a little girl, whom they named Lola. Coincidently, Lola was my mother's name. I sent Lola a gift and still kept in contact with him, thinking that if this meeting didn't happen, maybe it was for some reason. At this time, I was seeing the relationship differently; something too difficult. Although I ultimately remained with the desire to have met him in person, I trusted it played out the way it did for some unknown reason, which God would later reveal four months later when I met Sergio, the love of my life. I believe the French man was a sign for me to break free and take a chance at love again, somehow preparing my heart for what was to come.

Sergio

Sergio and Me

In July 2012, our group scheduled a night out at Caribbean Night Club, a club where a distinguished woman sang Spanish songs and a man played piano, both good friends of ours.

In addition, Waldo, (remember him?), would regularly climb on stage and sing, attending every week. After I broke it off with Waldo, I kept going to the club with my girlfriends. At that time, the woman who sang also did facials for a living, which I partook in occasionally. One day at her house, while she was finishing my facial, she shared with me,

"Last night at the Club, there was an extremely handsome man with dark hair and green eyes sitting at the bar. I casually mentioned that you and a group of girlfriends were there every Wednesday, but for whatever reason, this week you didn't attend. I asked him to come next Wednesday to meet you."

And he shrugged it off,

"Not sure I'll return."

She immediately added

"You have to return. You won't regret meeting this woman."

Once hearing this, I shared with her that I had no interest in meeting anybody, as I had just ended a relationship. She stressed,

"No matter, come looking fabulous. I'm sure he'll be there."

I wonder now if I ever thanked her for enticing me to go that night.

That Wednesday, my friends had been out of town, but my friend Normita, who you might recall lived with me in Puerto Rico years back, was living in Alabama at the time with her husband and daughter, who were visiting to possibly make a move to Miami. Since Normita loved to sing when she was young, I invited her to go out with me to the club where she could sing. She was embarrassed to sing in front of a crowd since it had been years since she did that. She reluctantly said,

"I don't know if I could do it."

In the end, and after much encouragement, she and her sister were excited to join me. Thus, we all went as planned on Wednesday to the Caribbean Night Club. I loved Normita for her loyalty and compassion. I miss our adventures.

While I was sitting with them at the table, the dark-haired, green-eyed man appeared. He casually sat down at the table behind us with a big group of his family. The moment he entered, I knew it was him. He sat, ordered his drink, and enjoyed being with his family. *Be still, my heart.* After some time had passed, he looked over to our table, and I waved at him. He stood and came over,

"Are you Vanessa's friend?"

I didn't hesitate,

"Yes."

He confirmed he was the man she was talking about and introduced himself as Sergio.

"I was here last week and they told me to come again, they said there was someone they wanted me to meet. I believe it's you."

I giggled like a school girl,

"Yes, it's me."

He nonchalantly returned to his table, and after a short time, he ordered a bottle of wine to our table. When I was leaving, he signaled me over, saying,

"There is a party at The Big Five in two months where Vanessa is selling tickets, and she wants me to buy some tickets. If you want to go with me, I'll buy them."

I hesitated, as a lady never accepts an offer rapidly,

"Let me check my schedule to see if I'll be available. Let's exchange numbers in order to plan."

I was hesitant, but enthralled and secretly giddy from the encounter.

Shortly after our introduction, Sergio began calling me. One day, he invited me to a Marlins' baseball game. The Marlins, Miami's pride and joy baseball team, had been dedicated to a new stadium, one which I had not visited. He excitedly shared he had tickets for Friday's baseball game, and he wanted me to join him. I immediately shared my interest in seeing the stadium, as I hadn't seen it, but mentioned I didn't wander out on Fridays. I explained to him that there was a group of my friends that gathered every Friday night at my house, causing me not to make other plans. I came up with a plan to go on Saturday, but unfortunately, he was working that day, in addition to the tickets being for Friday. Something made me say,

"Let me speak with the Dominoes group and I'll tell you if I can go."

It truly interested me in visiting the stadium, although I had never missed a game night with the boys, I was still mulling it over. I chatted with the group and explained what had happened, i.e.,

" I met this man, and he invited me to the Marlins' baseball game in the new stadium, which I really want to see."

They all agreed I should go and enjoy myself. I excitedly proceeded to call Sergio, cancel the Friday gathering, and accept his invitation. By the way, this was the first time I've ever canceled a Friday night Dominoes game. Those groups of guys loved me so much that, even being Oscar's best friend, they still wanted me to find happiness.

In my house, Dominoes was played religiously every Friday for over 20 years, of which Friday night Dominoes was never canceled, unless there was a death in the family. The Friday after Oscar had died and after we buried him, we didn't cancel a game night. Instead, we all went back to my house and gathered as if Oscar was there with us. We didn't play Dominoes that Friday night, we simply all sat together retelling stories, crying, and paying tribute to Oscar. All the group members were worried that with Oscar's death, Friday's gatherings would cease. I kept it going for Oscar's legacy and the boys loved me for that.

On that day, they kindly wondered if game night would be over. To put their fears to rest, I replied,

"No, you all can keep coming because, as Oscar would say, Dominoes is more my game than his."

It truly did entertain me more than it did Oscar. I would earnestly enjoy it when friends came to my house to party with us. I assured them they could keep coming every Friday. That is how it went. That Friday was the exception. I vowed to keep Oscar's memory alive as long as I could.

I went with Sergio to the Marlins game and had a wonderful time. Side note: there were three things I particularly liked about Sergio from the get-go. Firstly, the day I first met him in the restaurant, he made a kind gesture where he ordered us a wine bottle—those gentlemen's gestures of sending a wine bottle to tables have somehow fallen out with the times. Secondly, I noticed he was a family man; after all, he was there with his uncle and cousins, which warmed my heart. Lastly, the day he arranged to pick me up for the game at the stadium, he confirmed picking me up at 6:30 pm. As you have it, when the day came, he was picking me up at exactly 6:30 pm...punctual. That was a quality I adored, making it a plus. I am a Virgo after all. I knew at that moment this new love would be forever.

Shortly after the stadium game date with Sergio, we stayed in contact via telephone, speaking daily. He eventually asked me on a second date. Since I knew his day off was Friday and Fridays for me were Dominoes night, I decided to invite him over to play Dominoes and meet the gang.

"Do you like to play Dominoes?"

One of the things he always said was, *"Thank God I liked playing Dominoes"* because that's what pivoted our relationship to fruition. Being that since Friday was his day off, he liked to go out, he agreed to go. He enjoyed the group, the atmosphere, and had a great time, making him a regular every Friday and joining our gang. Sergio, from day one, did everything for my happiness. I loved that. I needed that.

Before I dated Sergio, I had planned a trip with my friends, Jacky and Sylvia, wherein we would travel to Canada for a week. I casually mentioned this to Sergio assuring him I would call him upon my return to continue our relationship. As it turned out, on the days I was in Canada, for one reason or another, I called him every day. The first day I called him was to get him to guide us to the waterfalls, since we were lost. After that, every night, I would call him to recount our day. I was hooked. He was the man who would love me till my death, this I was certain of. God just opened the other door for me.

When things are predetermined to happen, everything collides, creating a perfect union of peace, love, and tranquility.

He once confessed that if he didn't like Dominoes, he wouldn't have ventured into a relationship with me. He also liked the fact that I called him every day while in Canada, being that we really weren't exactly close. He never expected to have a serious relationship with me, especially since he had only been divorced a year and was not interested in a relationship (as I did), but our destiny was predetermined. We unwillingly began a relationship by attending gatherings such as The Big Five, an upscale event to which he had finally acquired tickets from Vanessa. The party was around three months after dating Sergio. When we attended that party, our relationship was solidified. When I say it was solidified, what I mean to say is that we were comfortable with one another, we liked each other, yet still not engaging in a physical relationship, all the while knowing something could happen. This is where it began, the story of my happy ever after.

A few days later, Sergio invited me to join him for a weekend getaway to Miami Beach, which I gladly accepted. We spent the weekend at a beautiful hotel in Miami Beach. Everything went perfectly. I felt at home. Sergio was attentive, gorgeous, decent, serious, funny and physically attractive. We both had an amazing time. At this point, our relationship had become quite serious. He continued coming to Dominoes night, sometimes staying the night. After a couple of months, his mother passed, giving me an opportunity to meet his family, albeit in a terrible situation. I met his kids and *everyone* for the first time at the funeral. One thing that Sergio mentioned that surprised him and a gesture he loved was when I decided to stay with him for the vigil. Sergio is an only child, and it pained me to see him going through this alone. Even though secondary family surrounded him, no one was going to stay the entire night with him while he mourned his mother. He looked torn apart, which is why I decided to stay with him, which he greatly appreciated. That night, our relationship blossomed stronger. They say trauma brings people together, but in our case, it was love.

His family was immensely kind. I tend to fall in love with my partner's family first, since I never really had a family of my own growing up. Families are attached to me. I noticed his family had a strong, united bond while being courteous and easygoing, which I truly admired. His children liked me, as did his family, which was important if our relationship was to last. In those candid moments, our relationship flourished. Our lives merged as one.

Sergio lived in an apartment, yet stayed several nights at my house, maybe going to his apartment once or twice a week. This lasted two or three years. He ultimately gathered the courage to ask to move in with me. He shared that it was a waste to keep paying rent for the apartment and me paying mortgage on my house, when he could move in and help pay the mortgage. Basically, he was ready to move in with me, but I was not. I didn't want to lose my *"independence"*. I stalled and stalled, he insisted and insisted. Until one day years later, I decided it was finally time for me to let go and let in. Therefore, on Noche Buena, when our families were gathered to celebrate, I surprised Sergio by giving him the keys to my house and lovingly asked him to move in and start a new life together. He, with the biggest smile ever, screamed *"YES!"* I've never seen a happier man. It was the best decision of my life.

The Pandemic "Covid-19"

{DIARY ENTRY}

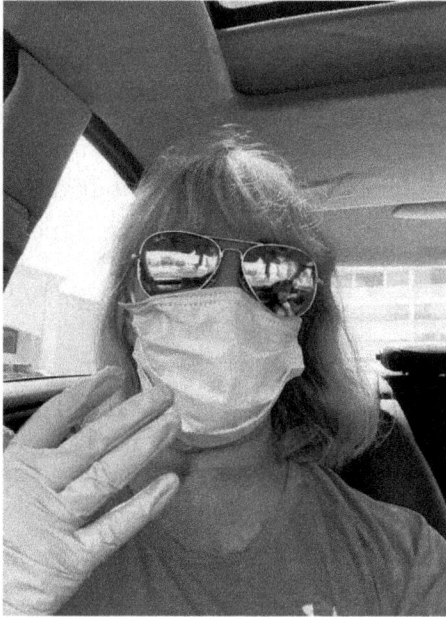

Me during the Pandemic

In 2020, the devastating COVID-19 pandemic was introduced to humankind, causing a mass division in the states, with people everywhere and wrought disaster and despair. The entire world was placed in quarantine, "imprisoned" in their homes. The beaches, stores, theaters, churches, everything was shut down. It endured, I believe, close to nine months. You weren't allowed to visit anyone, and nobody could visit you. The entire quarantine started strangely because we needed to curtail our life just to our house. No driving to the store, as a matter of fact, the only stores that were open were medical or emergency offices. There were some grocery stores opened, whose lines were around the corner and hours to wait in line and wearing a mandatory mask that makes you sweat years off. Life had morphed into the unknown, where people feared for their lives.

People started getting sick and not overcoming the illness. Some lost their lives, and many were alone when they passed, as they wouldn't allow family in the rooms to mourn with their loved ones. The world was scared and we were all lied to.

Our last day outside was on March 14, 2020, at Mojitos Restaurant, and on March 21st, I started to post. The lockdown lasted more than 60 days in total isolation.

As a form of staying connected with our family and friends during the pandemic, I began to post our daily activities on Facebook. This was what I wrote on that particular day:

Today on May 2nd, 2020, Day 50 of the lock-down/social distancing due to Covid-19.

Many of you are probably asking why I am documenting our daily activities. Well, I'll tell you why. In the coming years, I want to be able to remember how we kept our sanity during the Pandemic. Like happy hours, alone or with friends, going out to eat at different restaurants, visiting bars and clubs to listen to music, dance and mingle with our friends, planning a night at the Theater, mini vacations, or like we had planned for September, travel to Spain. We needed a reason to get up every morning and have something to look forward to. We decided to make a few improvements around the house, and this has proven to be very beneficial since we are exercising, getting a sun tan, keeping our minds focused on the work, and not gaining too much weight with all the food (that I normally do not cook.)

We still do our Happy Hours, we also listen to music and play games, which we love to do, and by posting it on my page, I am sharing it with you, my friends, and family, and it feels less lonely. I hope it also keeps you entertained following the progress of our activities. In the years to come, I hope there will be many for us (since this pandemic has taken so many people). I will see this on the memories that FB post and will never forget this trying time. I am grateful to have Sergio by my side, otherwise I would have gone mad being by myself. And that all my family and friends are still around as well.

Thanks for all the nice comments and likes. I hope this will end soon and that we can get together again.

Among all that chaos, Sergio and I managed to take full advantage of our time together and decided to renovate the house. We challenged our solitude by entertaining in card games, dominoes, cubilete, making drinks and randomly conversing about this or that, really just trying not to go crazy, day in, day out, in the house, us two, alone. Through quarantine, we managed to morph the house into a beautiful, serene enclave. Change was brewing. Life was fading into a new dawn. Everyone felt it.

A Happy Life

We all know in this life everything has a beginning and an ending, with some good stuff in the middle. Once Sergio moved, life flourished, and we began to create our new life together. Dominoes nights started becoming fewer and fewer until one day it came to an organic end, as most of the original members had passed on to a better life, meaning most of them died. In reality, only two or three people would show up by that time, diminishing the flavor of the game. I, with a heavy heart, decided to end Friday night Dominoes. I invited whoever wanted to come and prepared a speech to bid farewell to *"Bull's Inn."* It was an era that I will forever treasure and love.

An amazing thing about Sergio is his love for socializing and his extreme festiveness. He also enjoys traveling and as a matter of fact, thanks to his love for traveling, I've been able to travel to different places unknown to me prior to meeting him. Since our relationship dawned, we've seen Spain, Portugal, France, Greece, Alaska and Italy, visiting several different states in the United States.

As time went on, as time so does, Kelly and Nikki relocated to California with Dalton following a couple of years later, in pursuit of their dreams. A few years later, Huston married Cassie and remained in Miami, only seeing them randomly. Now there was only Huston left in Miami, and shortly after his marriage, we weren't able to maintain our weekly dinners, as they became enthralled with work and married life, like we all do. I still miss those weekly dinners till today. I continued to always reach out and reconnect our bond, but we were all living our separate lives. The waves of life ripple on.

In 2020, Huston and Cassie shared the news they were expecting a little bundle of joy. I was elated for them. Ultimately,

I believe that the separation of family weighed in on my decision to take the next step in life.

My family, I believe, is curious of the reasoning for my erratic change later in life, but I must disappoint and share no reasoning at all. I lived in Miami since 1978, and here we were in 2020, living in the same house for 30 years. The house I thought I would die in, or, as I would state,

"Con los peis pa' lante."

Meaning they would have to pry my lifeless body away from the house. As you may have ascertained, I really loved my little house, which was in a quaint neighborhood patrolled by an elderly Cuban guard who was overly flamboyant yet sweet as a peach. My house was the first in a lovely cul-de-sac with seven quaint houses surrounding it. I grew to love each and every one of those neighbors so much that we are still in contact today. At some point, Kelly lived two streets down on a different cul-de-sac, wherein my grandkids would come and visit me every day when they were growing up. Those were wonderful days. The neighborhood felt like home, with every house decorated for the holidays. Every year, the association would award me a prize for the best-decorated home in the neighborhood. I loved how rewarding it felt to set up the lights and ornaments and click on the lights to see how beautiful the house looked illuminated in the neighborhood.

On Halloween night every year, all the kids in the neighborhood would congregate at my house to wait for Kelly to lead them on to a night full of trick-or-treating. Kelly loved being with her kids and their friends. There were times I would join them and other times I would stay and give out candy to the kids with Oscar. The small streets were filled with families dressed in their scariest or best Halloween costumes. Huston, Dalton, and Nikki would get buckets of candies, which Kelly and I inspected before allowing them to eat. We would pose for pictures with all the kids in the neighborhood, all dressed in their costumes, while Oscar and I also donning a Halloween costume. I loved the sense of community and family it gave me. I loved my quaint cul-de-sac home in Poinciana. Back to why I changed everything....

One day, I had a dream I was visiting the Carolinas and remembered waking up happy and fulfilled, satisfied, you might say. Coincidently, Sergio had a cousin who lived in North Carolina in a small private area called *"Piney Creek"*.

I've never been there, but I had seen photos on Facebook of her reunions that she would post. It was recently after the Fourth of July when I saw photos depicting them on a river and having a wonderful time. For some reason those photos and the dream I had attracted me. I couldn't get that picture out of my head. They looked so happy. At night, while watching TV, without even thinking about it, I turned to Sergio and spouted,

"What would you think if we moved to North Carolina?"

He was surprised...

"Why not?"

I immediately asked him to call his cousin to ask the prices of the properties in that area. So he did. His cousin mentioned that Barbara, the other cousin, had recently purchased a cabin there. She was arriving from Miami and that we should get in contact with her to plan for a visit, especially since the tickets were only $49-$50.

I ran to the computer, searched for the flights, which were, in fact, $49, and turned to Sergio and asked if he could get a few days off work to visit Piney Creek. Sergio was excited, confused, but excited. I remember stressing that I was going on this trip merely to test whether I liked the area. I truly was not crazy about living in the country.

I tend not to think much about things. If I think too much about something, I won't do it. What the heart dictates at the moment, the heart does. We immediately booked our flight. Sergio and I had this conversation on July 5, 2020, and on July 9, 2020, we were on a plane to Piney Creek, North Carolina. Honestly, I can say my initial intention was to see what was there, but since I have always been one step ahead of myself, I had tucked a blank check in my purse. When we arrived at Sergio's cousin's house, again, I stated,

"I have to feel the place call my name. If it doesn't call to me, then para nada."

At the table, as we were conversing I turned to look at Sergio and give him the nod of *"Para nada"*. His cousin informed us she had a friend who was selling a cabin nearby by which has been listed for three years. She immediately called the realtor, and in the meantime, we also had a friend who was prepared to show us some properties. On our way to view the property, we drove down a scary curving road, which left me terrified, thinking I'd have to drive through this street every time. I was not interested and voiced my opinion, but we went anyway. As soon as I saw it I knew I didn't like it. I was losing hope.

The next day, Sergio's cousin drove us to see her friend's house. Upon driving towards the house and then once arriving, right away I felt something magical. Its beauty mesmerized Sergio and me, it captured us completely. We knew it was the house we wanted to spend the rest of our life in. Its pebble driveway led you to a two-story, picturesque Cabin with amazing views of the river lined with a white fence and robust trees and gardens with roaming deer. As a stroke of luck, this house was set for sale several times during those three years, but for one reason or another, it never happened. Afterward, I met the owner and curiously asked her why the house had never sold. Her answer astounded me, she said, "*Because the house was waiting for you and Sergio.*"

She was an extremely religious woman who longed for the house to find a family that truly loved the house and that was as happy as she and her husband were.

No matter why I decided to sell my home of 30 years in Miami and move to North Carolina, the truth is, it was destiny.

Nobody quite realizes how much power our subconscious mind encompasses. Subconsciously, we do things paying no mind to how we are doing them or are unaware that they were hidden away somewhere in our minds. This change in my life had everything to do with the thoughts held in my subconscious. The dream of having a wrap-around porch had been implanted for some time, much like a house with stairs. Every time I saw a Christmas movie, it delighted me to think I could one day decorate my own. The chimney was another idea planted in my subconscious, as I've always wanted my own chimney. I remember having a chimney in the house I bought in Chicago, but absurdly enough, I covered it and never used it. I can only assume that at that time, it didn't have much impact on my life. Years later, I dreamt of having one, where we would sit around the fire and have a lovely romantic night. Those small thoughts, which we neglect to realize, attract us and are deeply rooted in our subconscious. I would think those thoughts renewed the desire within to buy the cabin.

As soon as Sergio and I locked eyes, we knew this was exactly what we wanted, what we secretly longed for. I turned to Sita and asked her for the number of the realtor. I was determined to make an offer. Sergio was curious,

"What are you going to do with your house in Miami?"

Without a thought, I heard myself,

"Sell it."

Completely surprised, Sergio questioned,

"Sell it? Haven't you always said that was the house you would die in?"

God had other plans for me,

"Yes, but things change."

I was sure it was the right move. I saw my new life, and I wanted it.

The woman who owned it was more or less around my age, with her husband being 20 years her senior, and she had it for vacations. They lived half a year in Miami and the remaining half in North Carolina. She was desperate to sell it. I made an offer, a bit below asking, but she countered. I finally accepted and signed the contract. The contract was signed on July 11, 2020. The moment I glided my name on the paper, I saw myself celebrating every holiday in that house. I saw myself being *home*.

When we returned to Florida, the realtor who presented us with the cabin in North Carolina coincidentally was also a realtor in Miami. I mentioned to him I would need to sell the Miami property before purchasing the North Carolina property, and he assured me it would not be a problem and that he would sell it. We met and signed the listing agreement. On the next day, we had a buyer. It took one day to sell a home I've lived in for 30 years. We immediately went into overdrive. We needed to let go of everything in the house, because nothing would do in the new place. As a matter of fact, the house in North Carolina was being sold fully furnished. We didn't have to bring anything but our clothing. I couldn't believe all was falling into place, organically, as if it was destiny.

It was a grueling and exhausting two months of storing, selling, donating, and thrashing everything that didn't serve us. I can't begin to express how extremely intense those two months were. Needless to say, on September 1, 2020, we moved to North Carolina. Together, Sergio and I are ready to start our next journey.

Sergio and I in our North Carolina Home

Sergio is a loving, expressive, romantic man who loves me dearly. He might be the man who has loved me the most, and if perchance not, then he most certainly is the one who expressed it the most. Sergio tells me every day of my life that he loves me. Every single day. Every morning, he wakes me with a cafecito followed by a sweet kiss. We've had highs and lows, small and big discussions, due to our strong characters, but in the end, we grow together. He is a man of strong beliefs rooted deep in his personality and loves a good discussion. He has never liked me going to bed upset at him, he always comes to give me a kiss and makes sure I don't stay mad at him. I am not an easy person and am known to have a strong character as well. But we work well together.

Even at 76 years old, he makes me feel like an attractive and desirable woman. The moment he wakes up he turns to me and asks

"Why are you so beautiful?"

Those gestures complete me and fill me with his eyes of love. I know deep in my heart, he'll do anything for me. Every minute, he attempts to make me happy, and it works. Sergio has been wonderful to me and I couldn't have asked for a better ending to my book. I can say I have reached my goal and have found my happy ever after.

Our home in Piney Creek, North Carolina

Saying Goodbye

Me in front of our Poinciana home

On August 31, 2020, I closed the doors on my house in Poinciana for the last time, as we had been in a pandemic lockdown for three months. That moment was heart-wrenching. Memories played in my mind of all the wonderful moments lived in that precious little Poinciana home. Living in that house was the happiest and saddest time of my life. That was my home. A home where my grandkids grew from children to adults, a home where the kids were transformed, and where we celebrated births, baptisms, birthdays, Easter hunts, 4th of July fireworks, Halloween, Christmas Eve and Christmas, New Years, and death. Poinciana was home base. As I visited every room one last time, memories replayed in my mind of all the beautiful, marvelous moments shared together over the years in our treasured home. Poinciana, where Oscar lived his happiest years. I found myself crying, with joy, acknowledging I was truly blessed in having experienced profound joy and being able to take all those memories within my heart forever. Driving away, I saw my neighbors waving goodbye with tears in their eyes. I was leaving a piece of my heart and a big part of my history behind. I closed my eyes and saw that lonely covent girl leaving Cuba for a better life.

As Sergio and I were planning the dawn of our next chapter in the mountains, a new life was born into the family back in Miami. Huston and Cassie welcomed a beautiful little boy, named Grey, into the world. I imagined Oscar looking down at Huston and feeling like a proud dad up in heaven, sharing a big cigar with all the angels in his honor. That thought made me smile. Oscar would have adored Grey. Although the idea of leaving weighed heavy on me, I knew it was time for me to go.

The majority of people have dreams and aspirations in life. I didn't, really. I never lived having a dream, nor aspired to anything. I lived life as it was presented. As you have come to learn, I had horrible struggles as a little girl. I had to become the head of the family at the age of 23 with two kids to care for, which were my only main responsibilities and the number one priority that ignited me to move forward. Basically, I didn't dream, I lived, I struggled. The only real thing I ever wanted to do in life was to have my own family and find happiness. I realize I was unable to give my children a father and mother under one roof, but I most certainly did gift them my entire love, support, and guidance. I know I gave them everything that was within my reach, never lacking a roof over their heads, nor food, clothing, or schooling. I was fortunate to provide my kids with all the basic necessities through hard work and with love. I would have loved to give more, but I ultimately gave them all I could. I think that under the circumstances of our unstable life, they grew to be amazing adults achieving success-ful careers. Both of my kids are hard-working, good parents, and have created a beautiful family with extraordinary children. I am satisfied with the product of all the sacrifices in my life. In the end, I did achieve what I wanted: my happiness with a family, an amazing family that I am proud of, and, by the grace of God, healthy children, physically and mentally. *What else can a mother wish for?*

On September 1, 2022, we celebrated two years living in Piney Creek, North Carolina, two wonderful years of reforming our lives to a new environment, culture, and way of living. We are surrounded by a group of good people who have accepted us as one of their own and love us as family. We found our happiness, our community, and our family.

This year, we were fortunate to travel for a month to Europe and visit three different countries and 21 cities. It was a fantastic trip with friends, which will forever be in my heart. It allowed me to visit the birthplace of my ancestors, where I traveled to my father's home, where he was raised by his parents, my grandparents, in Asturias, Spain, and where my roots first grew. I thanked him while standing at his ancestral house and understood all his sacrifices. It all came full circle.

I'm fulfilled with this new life, not yearning for anything, only accepting joy as it comes, living a quiet life in the mountains, wherein I finally found my happiness. If I can reach it, you can too.

El Fin

My hope in writing this book is that my children will be able to comprehend that, although I was their mother, I was also young, alone, and attempting to maneuver through this life the only way I knew or could with limited knowledge. My main concern was avoiding making mistakes, which, in the end, was not avoidable, being human and all. Sometimes those mistakes come out just exactly how they should have. Life doesn't come with an instruction manual, and I didn't have all of life's answers, but what I did know is that I needed to do everything in my power to create a loving home for myself and my children, to be a caring mother, a responsible friend and a loyal wife. Yes, at times, as you've read in my story, things became messy, confusing, and exhausting, but at least we were doing it together. Isn't life exactly that? Leaving Cuba in search of a free life for my children was the best decision I could have ever made. I'm blessed and grateful for my children, spouse, family, friends, and grandkids, and for the many years I've been given the honor of living, and ultimately, writing this book.

All my experiences, sacrifices, and ventures have led me to share my story with the world. I hope that through these pages, you will challenge yourself to seek out what you dream of. Trust and live your best life. Write your own story. Find your way to happiness.

Top Left to Right: Dalton, Huston, Carlitos, Martica, Bryan, Melissa, Clara, Carlos
- Bottom Left to Right: Brandon, Kelly, Nikki, Michelle

www.ingramcontent.com/pod-product-compliance
Lightning Source LLC
Chambersburg PA
CBHW052035090426
42739CB00010B/1919